Immigrants don't eat dogs or cats.

Symbiosis of migration: Humans and non-humans one shared journey

Omar Albarracín

Published by: Ana Silvia Lara Publishing LLC
Editing · Layout · Publishing
@anasilvialara | www.anasilvialara.com/businessbestsellermastery

Index

Part I

CAUSES OF HUMAN AND NON-HUMAN MIGRATION

Part II

PSYCHOLOGICAL CONSEQUENCES OF MIGRATION

Part I II

MIGRATORY ECSTASY

Dedication

In memory of my brother

Luis María Albarracín Prieto,

exemplary educator, a teacher training teacher by vocation and a
graduate in Social Sciences,

who dedicated more than four decades

(40 years, 5 months and 11 days)

to the formation of generations in the city of Cúcuta, Colombia.

Teacher with a different pedagogical vision,

He planted the seed of self-criticism in his students,

free thought and commitment to a more conscious and just society.

His legacy transcends the classrooms he inhabited:

He was a human being of integrity, a great father, brother and son.

He also inspired us with his entrepreneurial spirit,

capable of opening new paths and infecting us all with his strength and passion for creating.

Today rest in the peace of the Lord,

but his mark remains indelible in the history that unites us

and in the dreams we still pursue.
- *Omar Albarracín*

Acknowledgments

This book is born from the intersection of invisible paths, from journeys that aren't always visible but are felt in the soul. It is a living testimony to the borders that try to divide us—and to the consciences that dare to unite what is separated.

To the luminous memory of Luis María Albarracín Prieto, an exemplary educator, a dedicated teacher training teacher, and a graduate in Social Sciences, who dedicated more than four decades—40 years, 5 months, and 11 days—to cultivating critical thinking in the city of Cúcuta, Colombia. A free-spirited teacher, a sower of ideas, an architect of generations.

In his classrooms, history wasn't just taught; consciousness was infused. Luis María courageously taught how to question, how to observe power, and how to think independently. He planted in each student the seeds of self-criticism, free thought, and a commitment to a more just and enlightened society.

But his legacy goes beyond the walls of the school: he was a person of integrity, a great father, brother, and son. His life was a silent example of dignity. He inspired us with his passion for teaching, but also for creating. With an entrepreneurial spirit, he paved the way where there were none, and he instilled in us his strength to build, transform, and never settle.

This book is also his. Because he migrated from teaching to transcendence. Because his words still dwell within us. And because his life reminds us that education is the first act of resistance against any form of injustice.

To all who migrate: people, animals, trees, souls. This journey is ours. One. Interspecies. Universal.

To those who dare to read with the eyes of the heart, thank you. May these pages not only inform, but transform.

To all migrants—human and nonhuman—who travel out of necessity, pain, destiny, or love, I offer this book as a song, a manifesto, and a living memory.

To the invisible energy that sustains us, to the language that frees us, and to the memory that never dies: eternal thanks.

Thank you for reading not only with your eyes, but with your soul.
Thank you for not being afraid of uncomfortable truths.
Thank you for sharing this journey with me.

Omar Albarracín
From the border where education sowed freedom, and migration ignited awareness

Preface

This is not a book to rush through. It's a book to feel, to pause, to recognize oneself in the other—human or nonhuman—and to dare to look beyond the boundaries imposed by fear, ignorance, or politics.

"Immigrants don't eat dogs or cats" isn't a provocation; it's a declaration of dignity. A phrase that became a defense against viral prejudice, but here it becomes a symbol of resistance, of love, of humanity.

This book is born from pain and hope, from forced exodus and the luminous possibility of rebirth. Omar Albarracín doesn't just write: he feels, observes, lives, and denounces. He delivers a manifesto of free thought, based on science, history, psychology, spirituality, and lived experience. He reminds us that migration is not just an economic or political decision: it's an evolutionary impulse. We migrate out of hunger, yes... but also out of love, curiosity, instinct, faith. And we don't migrate alone: animals, ecosystems, emotions, and memories migrate with us.

From Ulysses syndrome to the metaphor of the "Henhouse of Power," from the perspective of Frans de Waal and Darwin to the experience of the crocodile Pocho in Costa Rica, each chapter becomes a bridge between worlds we once thought were separate. Here, there is no victimhood or complaint; there is critical intelligence, symbolic depth, and uncompromising tenderness.

This preface is an invitation for you to read it with an open mind and an open heart. Active compassion. Because this book isn't just about those who cross deserts, jungles, or walls... It's about all of us who, at some point, have felt alienated, invisible, or displaced in our own land or body.

Prepare for a journey where the word is a map, the animal is a mirror, and the migrant is a prophet.

And when you close these pages, you can say, not only with your voice, but with your conscience:

" Immigrants don't eat dogs or cats. We eat dignity, a future, and dreams that don't fit within a border."

- Omar Albarracín

Introduction

The history of humanity is, above all, a history of migration. From the first *Homo sapiens* crossing a desert in search of water and life, to those who today cross oceans, continents—and even space—in the hope of a better future, migration has been much more than just moving: it has been a vital, spiritual, and evolutionary act.

This book isn't just about physical borders or personal grief. It reflects on the symbiosis of migration between humans and nonhumans. We are not alone on this journey: we share the planet, history, and destiny with them—the animals. We coexist. They are not inferior or alien, but evolving partners. They don't just feel pain, pleasure, or fear; they also express empathy, compassion, solidarity, and grief.

In this discussion on migration, we also talk about those who cross borders with us, those left behind, those whom humanity has domesticated, forgotten, sacrificed, and even loved.

From the controversial title *"Immigrants Don't Eat Dogs or Cats ,"* we propose a narrative that dismantles prejudices of discrimination and hatred and connects emotions. It opens paths toward new ways of inhabiting the world.

Immigrants are not a threat: we are hope. We don't come to destroy, we come to build. We transform, we are reborn, and we dare to dream of a more just world for all.

Part I: The causes of migration

We explore the drivers of migration: hunger, war, love, faith, persecution, climate change, the search for meaning.

We analyze current typologies: rural-urban, international, forced or voluntary migration, for economic, political, social, educational, ecological reasons... And, for the first time, space migration, that exodus to Mars that is no longer science fiction, but a real project of humanity.

The metaphors of "anti-democratic chickens" and "human crocodiles" help us understand the distribution of power, exclusion, and institutionalized selfishness.

From there, with the approach of primatologist Frans de Waal, we bring to the fore the power, empathy, and similarities between humans and nonhumans in their role within our shared evolutionary history.

Part II: Psychological consequences of migration

Delving into the psychological consequences of migration, we drew inspiration from the work of Spanish psychiatrist and researcher Joseba Achotegui, who has studied Ulysses syndrome, extreme stressors, and migratory grief.

Here the book becomes intimate, therapeutic and deeply human.

But it also becomes a denunciation:
What's the point of talking about human rights, power, or empathy if we don't protect migrants, those who are different, and outsiders?

Migration hurts: it hurts because of what we leave behind, because of the uncertainty, because of the loneliness. And that pain—shared by humans and nonhumans alike—unites us more than we think.

Part III: The Migratory Ecstasy

Here comes the hopeful turn: the moment when pain transforms into growth, and the migrant discovers a new version of themselves. Migration also reveals itself as a spiritual journey.

Inspired by Jesus—the outsider par excellence—three paths open up toward the civilization of the future:

1. **Return to Paradise:**
   A spiritual reconnection with God, with Genesis, and the promise of the Apocalypse. It is the search for the salvation of the soul and the rebirth of our original essence. Return home.

2. **The conquest of Mars:**
   A symbol of scientific advancement and the expansion of humanity. Migration is also colonization, but without repeating the mistakes of the past: bringing not only technology, but also awareness, empathy, and a new coexistence between humans and non-humans. A futuristic vision of what it would be like to live on Mars, as a new civilization.

3. **The society of the future:**
   A civilization rebuilt on education, compassion, equality, and respect for life and resources. A humanity capable of reinventing itself without having to leave the planet. Able to live in peace, to collaborate, and to integrate true human values.

A humanity where we can all shout, with one voice and with dignity:

"IMMIGRANTS DO NOT EAT DOGS OR CATS."

Scan the following QR code by Bayron Omar Albarracín Monsalve:

Part I, causes of human and non-human migration

CHAPTER I

Evolutionary process of humans and non-humans: a single journey

When we talk about the human evolutionary process, we connect directly with migration. Therefore, migration is one of the consequences of our evolutionary success. The 100,000 years we have been away from our African cradle have allowed us to evolve into what we are today.

According to the evolutionary tree of the human genus, including the four great apes—the orangutan, gorilla, bonobo, and chimpanzee—and based on DNA comparisons, the numbers indicate that bonobos and chimpanzees form a single genus, *Pan.* The human lineage split from *Pan 's ancestor* about 5.5 million years ago. Some scientists believe that chimpanzees, bonobos, and humans are close enough to form a single genus, *Homo.* Since chimpanzees and bonobos split about 2.5 million years ago, after their common ancestor split from our lineage, they are equally close to us. Gorillas split earlier, and the orangutan split even further back, about 14 million years ago.

One hundred thousand years ago, when *Homo sapiens* was just beginning to walk the earth, climates were more extreme, dangers more evident, and death was a neighbor lurking in the caves. However, amidst this uncertainty, something powerful began to take shape: a silent alliance, an unexpected symbiosis between species that, when they met, would change their destiny forever.

Around the campfires, our ancestors noticed the presence of many animals, including dogs and cats. They noticed that the wolves' presence was somewhat different: they didn't flee, they didn't attack, they just watched. Perhaps they were individuals who had been expelled from their pack. Perhaps they were the most curious... or the hungriest. Little by little, without any agreement, without words or gestures, these wolves began to approach humans, not as prey or predators, but as companions. In exchange for scraps, they warned of danger. In exchange for warmth, they offered loyalty.

Thus began a shared journey: humans domesticated the dog, and the dog domesticated the human. Because it wasn't just humans who changed the wolf; the wolf also changed humans. A symbiosis formed between them. *Symbiosis,* taken from biology, means "living together"; that is, in a close, beneficial, and coevolutionary relationship. These relationships between humans and non-humans have been fundamental to survival throughout history, as well as to the emotional, cultural, and spiritual development of our species.

Charles Darwin, in *The Descent of Man, and Selection in Relation to Sex* (1871), argued that humanity is no exception to evolution and that many of our social behaviors are rooted in instincts we share with other animals. These social instincts—such as cooperation, fairness, and empathy—have evolved because they offer advantages to the survival and reproductive success of individuals and groups.

Migration for humans and non-humans

Migration, for both humans and non-humans, is a parallel and symbiotic process. Human migration refers to the movement of people from one place to another, either within a single country or between countries, with the purpose of settling temporarily or permanently in a new destination. This phenomenon can be caused by various factors, which we will discuss in this first part of the study. The important thing to note is that migration has been a constant in the evolution of human societies, contributing to cultural exchange and the development of civilizations.

Migration in non-human animals is defined as the periodic and seasonal movement of certain species from one habitat to another, generally in response to changes in environmental conditions, food availability, or reproductive needs. This behavior is common across diverse groups and affects all biodiversity, including birds, mammals, fish, reptiles, amphibians, insects, and even the plant kingdom.

Both humans and non-humans migrate for survival, for the need to adapt, and for the instinct to protect their loved ones. Although we might think the animal doesn't fully understand where it's going, both, deep down, are seeking the same things: safety, food, companionship... a place where they can feel at home again.

Both are capable of building a home wherever they go: humans adapt to new countries, new languages, new cultures, customs, and trades. Non-human animals learn new paths, new routes, new beds, new voices. Both are driven by an inner drive: they are architects of hope.

The three faces of migration: internal, external and spatial

Did you know that the animal holding the record for the world's longest migration is the Arctic tern? This seabird travels approximately 96,000 kilometers (60,000 miles) annually on its route from the Arctic to the Antarctic and back. Over the course of its lifetime, its journey is equivalent to four round trips to the Moon. Like human migrants, the Arctic tern is a symbol of resilience and adaptation, facing storms, extreme climates, and the constant uncertainty of its path. Its story reminds us that the journey is not always easy, but in every flight lies the search for a home and the hope of survival.

In this section of the study, we will review the types of migration, with an updated perspective on our contemporary reality. We discuss internal, external, and spatial or planetary migration. These are concepts that allow us to explore the deeper layers of the phenomenon. It is not just a physical change from one place to another, but an emotional and cultural journey that redefines the migrant and the communities with which they interact.

These categories illustrate how human and non-human displacement—whether within a country, to a foreign territory, or, seen metaphorically (or perhaps as a very close reality), outside our planet—shares a common root: the need to live better.

Internal migration

In the beautiful countryside of Colombia, where the golden hues of the sunset paint the sky and the wind carries the whisper of the mountains, lived María, an 18-year-old peasant girl. Her life was tied to the land, working since she was a child alongside her family in corn and bean fields. However, the tranquility of her home was shattered when the guerrillas arrived in the area. In their fight to dominate the territory, they forced her family to make a painful decision: to abandon their village and migrate to the city in search of a better life.

Internal migration occurs when there is movement within the borders of a single country, generally from rural areas to cities, or between regions, departments, or states. It is commonly driven by economic, social, violence, or environmental factors.

From a parallel perspective, just as humans migrate for survival or better opportunities, animals also migrate, facing human-created barriers. Urban expansion can dispossess animals of their habitats, forcing species to coexist in shared spaces, often in tension.

When adapting to a new culture, internal migrants often feel like they are leaving their roots behind while trying to integrate into a dominant urban culture. Psychologically, this shock can cause anxiety and stress, which we will discuss in more detail in Part II of the study on the consequences of migration.

External migration

Olga was 32 years old when the war reached her town in eastern Ukraine. Until then, she had led a simple life: she worked as a music teacher at an elementary school and spent her weekends caring for her sick mother and watering the small garden behind their house. Everything changed in a matter of days. Explosions began to get closer, and the school closed indefinitely. The markets were empty, the streets were filled with barricades, and the air smelled of gunpowder. The decision to leave wasn't easy. Her mother refused to leave their home, clinging to the memories of a life built within those walls. Olga had to leave alone. Heartbroken, she vowed to return for her and took a crowded train to Poland. She didn't know where she would go next, but her mind was focused on a single goal: finding safety for both of them. Upon arriving in Warsaw, she found a reception center filled with people of all ages. Some spoke her language, others didn't, but they all shared a common sadness. Over time, he got a job in a cafe, learned some Polish, and found a place to live with his mother. Today, he leads a stable life in that city, achieving perhaps the greatest success of an immigrant: living safely and freely.

External migration is international displacement, crossing borders in search of safety, better opportunities, or survival. Those who leave their country face the so-called "double absence," in which they feel completely separate from either the country of origin or the host country. This generates emotional conflicts such as nostalgia and migratory grief, which we will analyze later, based on the studies of psychologist Joseba Achotegui.

This phenomenon has multiple causes: wars, political persecution, economic crises, natural disasters, forced displacement, invasions... Wars have been one of the main causes of international migration. Olga's case is an example of how the war between Ukraine and Russia in 2022 transformed the lives of thousands. Each migrant carries with them a unique universe of experiences and hopes. Olga, like so many others, faced displacement, loss, and uncertainty, but found ways to rebuild her identity in a new place.

There's always a way out. There are always options. We are always protected by God.

Spatial migration

Lia looked back at Earth from the ship's window for the last time. She had grown up in a city by the sea, where every afternoon the sun dyed the waves orange and the wind carried the scent of salt. She never thought the day would come when she would leave her home—

not to move to another country, but to abandon the planet altogether. Her grandfather had told her stories of his own migration: "We left our village when I was a child," he said. "We had no choice. We learned a new language, found a new home, and never went back."

Now it was Lía's turn to embark on a journey of no return. The Earth was collapsing: wars, environmental pollution, global warming, human selfishness, biological aggression, unbreathable air, birdless skies, and water scarcity. Humanity, as always, refused to give up. If in the past they had crossed seas and mountains, now they would cross space. Lía was not alone. Thousands of settlers like her were traveling to Mars, a barren rock they would one day call home. She knew that adaptation would be difficult, that gravity was different, that the air had to be manufactured, but she also knew that she was part of a new civilization, more empathetic, less narcissistic. She knew that humankind had always been migrants. From African tribes to navigators without maps, migration has always been an act of survival and faith.

Talking about migration is no longer limited to movement within the same country, between cities, or between continents. This trend is changing. Figures like Elon Musk are actively promoting the possibility of a million people migrating to Mars by 2050. This isn't a futuristic whim, but the extreme consequence of a world collapsing under the weight of its own mistakes.

The causes are multiple: climate change, natural disasters, water scarcity, rising sea levels, pollution, intolerance, distorted politics, selfishness, dehumanizing competition, overpopulation, wars. In many regions of the world, life has become unsustainable for both humans and nonhumans. In this context, migrating off-planet seems a legitimate option.

Seen from another perspective, spatial migration also represents a need to transcend, to create a new civilization. We will explore this further in Part III, toward the end of this study, when we address the migratory ecstasy.

It could be a great opportunity to restart humanity, even if it also entails risks: adaptation to gravity, lack of oxygen, bone disintegration.

Many will be willing to take that risk, to make a contribution—not just intellectual, but vital—to the construction of a new world.

We cannot live without our fellow planetmates. Scientifically, there is still no conclusive evidence that nonhuman animals can accompany us on this journey. However, some microorganisms might initially do so. So the question arises: Will we bring animals to Mars for our benefit or as symbolic equals? Will they migrate with us as resources or as companions?

A new ethical debate arises here:
If we're going to start over... will we continue to dominate others, or will we build a more empathetic and fair relationship?

CHAPTER 2

Immigrants don't eat dogs or cats.

No! Immigrants don't eat dogs or cats;
we eat dignity between courses! We eat goodbyes!
We eat faith, we eat tomorrow, even if we don't know what! I am the
son of corn, the grandson of the jungle, the one who walks with the
dog and the cat, the one who doesn't give up...! They call us a
problem, but the real burden is the system. They wipe us off the map,
they take us from the ground, and yet we sow the future in grief. We
are the land that crosses the seas, we are the pulse of the heart. We
don't eat dogs or cats, gentlemen, we bring work, culture and love!

Migration has become highly politicized today; it has become a topic of global discussion. In some countries, it is used as an electoral or partisan rhetoric, both to defend their territories and to win voters. Unfortunately, in this wave of migration over the last four years in the United States, unscrupulous individuals have arrived who have damaged the image of all immigrants: criminal gangs like the Tren de Aragua (Venezuela), common crime, human trafficking, drug trafficking... and, most recently, Haitians are eating their pets.

This comment originated from unfounded information that went viral on social media and was shared on the X network. It claimed that Haitian migrants, recently settled in Springfield, Ohio, were eating their neighbors' pets.

It all begins in Ohio, in a town called Springfield. According to the 2020 census, approximately 60,000 people lived there, in old Victorian houses with a mini-Chicago feel and great architectural beauty. Suddenly, many Haitians began arriving. It is estimated that nearly 20,000 have arrived in the last four years, which means that for every four residents, one is Haitian.

They didn't arrive illegally: they arrived protected by temporary status, fleeing a country riddled with violence. They currently enjoy immigration status that allows them to work. Springfield needed labor for hard jobs that local residents didn't want to do—especially in factories, manufacturing, and heavy labor from sun up to shade.

They arrived and spread the word: there are jobs and opportunities in Springfield. Furthermore, since they weren't undocumented, they could access free medical care. By 4 or 5 a.m., they were already forming long lines outside clinics seeking medical services.

Comments began circulating on Facebook that Haitians were stealing ducks from parks, decapitating them, and eating them. A photo even appeared of a Haitian man carrying a duck by the neck, presumably to eat it. This was the first spark that fueled the rumor that Haitians were eating the village's animals.

Speaking of ducks, and since this study is about defending animals, we remember that many of them become so closely related to us—humans—that they align with us in ways of interspecies survival and understanding. This space also serves to point out that in many countries, organizations and laws prohibit the production of *foie gras*. This practice consists of inserting tubes into the throats of ducks and geese several times a day to force-feed them enormous quantities of corn and fat. Their livers swell to ten times their size. These birds are then slaughtered, and their livers are sold at exorbitant prices as *a luxury dish*.

Ducks are also being bred in laboratories so they don't make sounds and cause stress to their caregivers. All this to facilitate their exploitation. Apparently, Haitians aren't the only ones who kill and eat ducks. Animal exploitation, whether in parks or factory farms, is equally cruel and unnecessary.

Taking a duck from its natural habitat—a park, a pond, or from its single-file parade in front of our homes—is illegal. But so is imprisoning it, force-feeding it, and killing it. Both cases should be questioned.

Back in Springfield, some time later, someone posted a photo on Facebook of a dead cat hanging from a tree in a house inhabited by Haitians. No one knows if it was killed, why it was there, or if the cat died of natural causes. But it was enough to fuel more rumors: *Haitians eat dogs and cats.*

Our perspective in this study is not political, but rather an analysis of the symbiosis between humans and nonhumans, with reciprocal processes of support, coexistence, and evolution. In this case, the symbionts are:

– Those who arrive (migrants)
– Those who are (natives)

Migrants must respect ecosystem norms, species conservation, and the laws of the host country—in this case, the United States. But residents must also recognize the contribution migrants make to their economy, culture, and social fabric.

The issue of pets must be addressed by the authorities, who have already expressed their views. It would be outrageous if people resorted to such extreme acts as eating these animals. This has only happened in situations of war, hardship, or survival, such as Uruguayan Air Force Flight 571, which crashed in the Andes in 1972, and whose survivors had to feed on the bodies of their deceased companions.

Some newscasts interviewed Springfield residents. One woman showed a pond where there used to be many ducks, but now there are no more. However, local authorities denied any evidence that Haitians had eaten them. Even the governor spoke about it.

Haitian residents reported being afraid to leave their homes, go to the market, or seek help. One man said they don't eat those types of animals; their diet includes beef, goat, chicken, and fish. A Mexican woman interviewed said Haitians are entrepreneurial and have taken advantage of the city's job opportunities.

Many of them received death threats and racist phone calls urging them to leave. Some schools and buildings were evacuated due to bomb scares. The local mayor stated that some citizens were frustrated by the 20 to 25% population growth in just four years, which put pressure on infrastructure and social services. But he also acknowledged the productive and human contribution of Haitian migrants.

In short, Haitians—like other immigrants—do not eat dogs or cats.

This analysis addresses how, in the struggle for power, politicians use phrases and rumors to influence the electorate. Migration has become a central focus of campaigns and speeches, especially in host countries like the United States.

A country that, despite its history of slavery, indigenous displacement, and structural racism (such as the Jim Crow system), has also been an example of overcoming. However, social residues persist. A Harvard article collects testimonies from African Americans and Hispanics in New York who could not easily board taxis. Councilman James Sanders recounted:

"After waiting 45 minutes and seeing 20 taxis go by, I realized something was up. One driver refused to take me and drove 20 more feet to pick up a friendly white couple."

Racism isn't dead. It's just learned to disguise itself.

And that's why this book exists.
To repeat out loud: Immigrants don't eat dogs or cats! We eat faith!
We eat dreams!
We eat humanity!

Who migrates more: men or women?

Globally, migration patterns show that, although historically men migrated in greater proportion, female migration has increased significantly in recent decades. According to recent data, the International Organization for Migration's (IOM) *World Migration Report 2024* indicates that women represent approximately 48% of the world's migrant population, although in some regions—particularly

Latin America, the Caribbean, and Eastern Europe—they represent up to 50%.

The gender migration flow has a dimension determined by socioeconomic, cultural, and political factors. Traditionally, men migrated first in search of economic opportunities, leaving their families behind with the intention of sending remittances or reuniting in the future. However, the situation is changing, and today many women migrate on their own, driven by the search for employment, education, family reunification, or the need to escape violence and discrimination in their countries of origin.

The growing participation of women in global migration is linked to the rise of independent women, the women's revolution, and advances in gender equality in various areas. Some of these factors have directly influenced this phenomenon and have allowed women to make the decision to migrate independently. Historically, women have been more closely tied to the domestic sphere, while men were the ones who migrated. However, with globalization, significant changes have emerged in these behavioral patterns. Fortunately, women have been able to achieve a social transformation that has changed these paradigms.

Education itself, as we have already mentioned in other areas, is one of the strong foundations for a society's development. Female education has provided women with greater employment opportunities and empowerment, allowing them to seek new horizons outside their country of origin, if necessary.

But the news isn't always so good or encouraging. Women continue to be undervalued and mistreated in many societies around the world. Women still face severe oppression due to deeply rooted religious, political, and cultural factors. Although many countries have made progress toward gender equality, in others, discrimination and lack of rights persist, limiting their autonomy and opportunities for development.

CHAPTER 3

Metaphor of anti-democratic chickens

As a six-year-old boy, Norwegian zoologist and psychologist Thorleif Schjelderup-Ebbe received a flock of hens from his mother. Soon, each hen had a name. He became fascinated by their behavior. A little later, at the age of ten, he began to take notes on their actions. He kept a record of how many eggs his hens laid each day, which one pecked which, and began to identify exceptions within the vertical hierarchy. He was the first person to describe a pecking order among hens, which he called the pecking order.

He visualized that the hierarchy was given in a triangular form, like this:

- Hen A dominates and pecks hen B.
- Hen B dominates and pecks hen C.
- Hen C dominates and pecks hen A.

This study gave rise to what we now know as the pecking order, which we will adapt metaphorically here to understand how a so-called democratic state works.

We want to reaffirm, through this metaphor, how in a system called democracy, a triangular power system is wielded, always circulating among the same forces: the circle of power, which revolves with the constant intention of dominating the people. The people are the hens most affected by the system.

These hens are the ones with the least participation. The only way to peck is through voting, but within a system controlled by a higher authority. This produces social breakdown, closely linked to the causes of migration, directly impacting people's lack of opportunities for advancement within their social structures.

In true democracies, people don't just deliberate and choose; they also decide. This frustration with a closed, hierarchical system leads many to decide to leave their communities, and thus migration occurs.

Structure of a democratic government with pecking order

We will review an example of how a democratic state structure is established, comparing it with the hierarchical triangulation of power—known as the pecking order—in a society, as explained by Thorleif Schjelderup. One of the shortcomings of democratic systems of government is human inequality, both at the individual and collective levels, which causes injustice, limits development, and pushes people to leave their countries due to a lack of equal opportunities and rights in key areas such as education, health, gender, ethnicity, religion, thought, among others. This can generate multiple disparities and profound impacts.

Chicken coop of power

- (A) Political parties and/or economic elites dominate
- (B) the presidents and/or heads of government, who in turn dominate
- (C) the bureaucracy, which ends up dominating (A) the political parties.

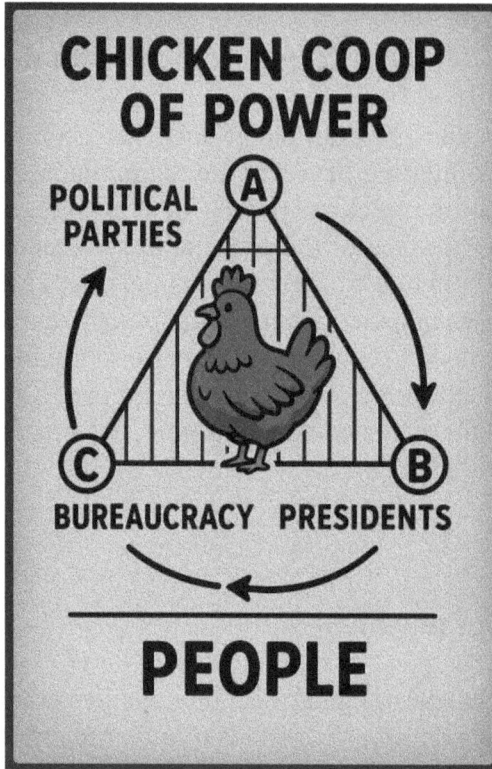

CHICKEN COOP
OF POWER

POLITICAL (A)
PARTIES

(C)   (B)
BUREAUCRACY PRESIDENTS

PEOPLE

Our intention in this study is not to directly impact politics. But, as we progress, we realize that it is unavoidable. In light of positions and systems that operate under a triangular structure—called democracy—this metaphor illustrates how domination flows among the "stronger hens," in a feedback loop of unequal power. Control remains between homogeneous forces that negatively impact the weaker hens: the people. These are the ones with the least participation. Their only way to "peck" is through voting, within a system controlled from above.

This model produces social breakdown, closely linked to the root causes of migration. In true democracies, decisions are made, not just deliberation and choice. But when that possibility doesn't exist, frustration drives many to leave their communities.

In the most advanced societies, where voters are no longer bought with a bag of cement or paving a street during election time, economic wars, high tariffs, exclusion of migrants, and protectionist policies are offered. Yet, the people—the chickens outside the circle—remain the most affected and subject to decisions made by others.

In a chicken coop, there's an ALPHA hen, who can peck everyone else without retaliation. She pushes the others out to take her place. Then there are the intermediate-ranking hens, who can peck those lower in the hierarchy, all the way down to the weakest, who can't peck anyone. The people are those excluded hens, located at the bottom of the power triangle. However, the three groups of ALPHA hens need them to sustain themselves in the "jam" of benefit sharing, which only those who are part of the flow enjoy.

The triangular flow of power

This triangular flow of power directly impacts the well-being of all of us who live in that corral.

- (A) At the top, political parties and/or economic elites act as gatekeepers to power. They fight, betray each other, finance campaigns, support those most likely to win, manipulate from the shadows, and then recoup their investment through contracts and favors. They are the masters of the nibbles.
- (B) On the second level are the presidents or heads of state, the hen who clucks and screams the most during their term. They like being on top so much that many repeat or perpetuate their positions, even changing constitutions. Some bow down to their sponsors—parties or elites—others defy them. That's how the henhouse works: alliances, betrayals, fierce public debates... and reconciliations in the next campaign. This "sophisticated

empathy" is difficult for the people to understand, but it's part of the pecking order: the rules of the political henhouse.

- (C) At the third level is bureaucracy, which often serves the system more than the citizenry. Parties may change, presidents too, but bureaucracy remains. This anchor gives it structural power: it handles information, rules, procedures, and execution. It is not just a passive executor; it is a political actor with the capacity to shape, condition, or sabotage visible power. In this metaphor, bureaucracy is the invisible anchor that balances—or unbalances—the game between chickens A and B.

Meanwhile, the people watch from the sidelines, their only capacity for pressure limited to protests, elections, and social organization, but within a system that has been designed to perpetuate the pecking order.

Is another chicken coop possible?

This human chicken system would work better if there truly existed a symbiosis of mutual aid, where everyone was a protagonist within society. But this mutualism breaks down: political power oversteps the boundaries of citizen protection and, in many societies, turns into parasitism.

In a true democracy:

- (A) The people are the highest authority, with mechanisms such as referendums, citizen initiatives, petitions and popular control.
- (B) Representatives and government (Executive and Legislative branches): president, prime minister, Congress or Parliament.
- (C) Institutions, bureaucracy and justice (Judicial Branch and Public Administration).

In this model, the people cannot be the defenseless base of the pyramid. It's not just about voting, but also about monitoring, questioning, demanding, and changing their leaders. Constitutions must ensure that power does not become a fiefdom. Public opinion, a free press, and citizen participation bodies must act with real force.

The exit from the henhouse

The only way to break the coop is:

- Do not allow dictatorships.
- Have a solid political education.
- Demand transparency and accountability.
- Strengthen citizen participation.
- Alternate power and return it to the people.

In a true democracy, the people are not the hen who receives the final peck, but the rooster who crows and decides the course of the henhouse. Power must always return to the people. If these formulas are not followed, if the henhouse becomes a cage, if the pyramid no longer represents the people, then many have no choice but to migrate in search of another henhouse that will shelter them.

Allegory of the human crocodiles

Omar Albarracín

This is a true story about the incredible friendship between Gilberto "Chito" Shedden, a Costa Rican fisherman, and a crocodile named "Pocho." In 1989, Chito found Pocho, seriously wounded with a gunshot wound to the eye, lying agonizing on the banks of the Reventazón River, after a rancher had shot him in the head for attacking his cattle. Instead of abandoning him, he decided to care for him. For months, he fed him chicken and fish, gave him shelter, and even slept beside him for warmth and security. Against all odds, Pocho not only survived but also developed a deep bond with Chito. Years later, when Chito tried to free him, Pocho followed him home, demonstrating a bond that went beyond simple dependence on food. Together, they starred in a spectacle for more than two decades. The two shared a unique friendship that attracted the attention of tourists and international media. They performed weekly shows in Siquirres, where they demonstrated their trust and affection for each other. Pocho passed away of natural causes on October 12, 2011, leaving a legacy of wonder and admiration in Costa Rica and around the world.

This true story reinforces the idea that the symbiotic relationship between humans and nonhumans is not based solely on dominance and utility, but can include empathy, collaboration, respect, and even genuine affection. Furthermore, during migration, many immigrants experience something similar with animals: they find in them companionship, refuge, and an emotional bridge between the past and the present.

Like Pocho, many migrants arrive wounded by circumstances: displaced by violence, poverty, or lack of opportunities, as we'll see later in the different causes of migration and the psychological consequences to which we can be exposed. Chito, in this case, represents the solidarity, welcome, and care that some find in their new destinations. But there's also a double meaning: not all migrants find a "Chito" along the way; many end up in the jaws of a human crocodile ready to exploit them.

The crocodile is a patient predator. It lurks beneath the motionless water, its eyes barely visible above the surface. It doesn't attack immediately: it waits, letting its prey approach confidently, with the illusion of having found refuge, until, at the right moment, it pounces with its relentless jaws. It doesn't kill instantly. No. The crocodile drags its prey underwater, subdues it, twists it until it is disoriented, until its resistance vanishes. Only then does it begin to devour.

In the jungle of migration, human crocodiles also lurk

They don't live in rivers, but in businesses, hotels, offices, farms, restaurants, and factories. They don't roar or growl, but their voice is a seductive whisper:
"There's work for you here."

Its prey arrives hungry, in need, with the urgency to survive, full of dreams, ready to take on challenges it can't even imagine. Ready to give it its all. And the crocodile knows it.

He doesn't have to attack immediately. He lets him in. He lets him believe he's found solid ground. That he can start over. But he soon tightens   his   grip:
"You don't have papers, you're a migrant... so this is what it is."

Grueling days. Endless work. Poor pay. Unrelenting abuse.

" Shakira, Shakira, rigid force, 7:30, the alarm has gone off, I want to be in bed, but it can't be done, I have to get the kids home at nine. Same coffee, same cooking, same old stuff, same routine, another shitty day, another day at the office. I have a shitty boss who doesn't pay me well, I walk in and he drives a Mercedes-Benz, he's got me as a recruit. The son of a bitch..."

(Composition: Shakira, Edgar Barrera, Keityn and Kevin Mauricio Cruz)

The modern crocodiles of the human jungle don't tear flesh, but they do tear dignities. They don't sink bodies in water, but they submerge souls in fear. They are experts at reading broken emotions. They sell hope disguised as opportunity. They live off the needs of others, repeating them like a cycle. They present themselves with fake smiles, poised and friendly. It's definitely not possible to generalize, but they exist... they do exist.

And I say this with experience: they're not always native or indigenous. Sometimes they're other migrants who are just a step ahead of us. They arrived earlier, learned the system, knew the cities, the language... and now they've shed their prey for predator. Because in this jungle, whoever survives longest learns to hunt. The food chain is unforgiving. And so, the new migrants enter the river, unaware that the water is full of gaping jaws.

Hope is not dead: Chitos and Pochos also exist

There's good news. There's a counterpart to these lurking human crocodiles. Humanity is full of Chitos and Pochos.

They are those who accompany, protect, and lift up.
They are those who build paths across the abyss.
They don't give charity: they sow belonging. They welcome with kind words, with simple gestures, with respect for the history of others.
They know that a greeting can save an afternoon. They know that an opportunity can change a destiny.
A "yes" can change a life.

They are a steady light. They guide without invading. They listen without judging. They accompany without imposing. They give direction without demanding obedience. These are good people. These are good companies.

It's worth highlighting here some people who contributed to and sheltered my family. Like the Costa Ricans, "los ticos" Fernando and Sonia Tapias, wonderful, kind-hearted people who opened their homes at a crucial moment in our lives, becoming a guide and emotional support. Especially at the beginning of the migration process, when everything is uncertain and our hearts are heavy with nostalgia. A sincere prayer to the mighty God, and a morning cup of coffee, connect the soul with something greater, forming a shield and courage to face the world.

Like other individuals and businesspeople in Tampa, friends like Julián Torres, Colombian entrepreneurs Fabio Orozco, Juan C. Restrepo, and his manager Henry Correa.
In Saint Petersburg, Marlon Yepes.
Cuban Sergio and his wife, Colombian Paula Curbelo. In Clearwater, David Nieves and Diana Durango.

All these people and their companies are much more than that minority in the jungle. To all of them, thank you so much.

We meet these good people every day along the way. They open doors for us. They feel compassion and admiration. They know that we, migrants, are a powerful and unstoppable force. We're going all out.

We are the beacons and the trees that bloom on the riverbank. We give our all with the intention of contributing and moving forward.

Because migrating isn't an act of weakness:
It's a leap of faith.
It's walking into the unknown, with hope...
and God's help as your only luggage.

CHAPTER 4

Main causes of migration

In this section, we'll expand on valuable information regarding the causes of migration. We'll delve deeper into the human aspect, which is one of the focuses of this study, without neglecting—albeit briefly—what causes the migration of some nonhumans, our fellow planet members. They truly have no borders: they are free to move, as humans surely should be.

We focus on everything that migration can cause from different perspectives, both for the two protagonists of this discussion—humans and nonhumans—who undoubtedly represent us in our personal experiences or those of those close to us. It's very difficult for any of us not to have interacted with someone who wants to migrate, who has already migrated, or who is an immigrant. Drawing on that experience, we aim to analyze the many factors that influence this decision. At the same time, we aim to encapsulate how nonhumans are part of this inevitable relationship with us, humans.

Imagine a community in an agricultural region that depends on the rainy season to grow corn. But, due to overexploitation of groundwater and climate changes, the crops no longer thrive. Young birds begin to migrate to the cities, while birds that used to nest in nearby lands also abandon the area, seeking refuge in more fertile wetlands.

Economic causes

The economic causes of migration can be considered part of the historical and current driving force of human displacement, highlighting how they are rooted both in our survival instinct and in the inequalities of the global system. Throughout time, human beings have sought not only food, water, and shelter, but also opportunities for well-being and progress.

Globalization has created an interconnected but deeply unequal economy. While some regions concentrate capital, technology, and decent employment, others are forced to export their labor as if it were just another product, or simply to give away their labor to foreign investors. This dichotomy turns migration into an act of modern survival.

Search for opportunities

What for us humans represents opportunities, employment, salary, or social mobility, for non-humans can mean access to food, favorable temperatures, and security.

Let's look at two extreme cases:

New York vs. Bangladesh

New York, United States. Iconic city. Picturesque at first glance, full of lights, skyscrapers, and dollars. But beneath the postcard image is a city full of immigrant cooks working 12 or more hours a day, without papers. Cleaners, security guards, restaurant, hotel, and construction workers. Men and women who send remittances without knowing if they'll be able to pay the rent at the end of the month.

On the other hand, Bangladesh, "the land of rivers," whose capital is Dhaka. According to the World Bank, its estimated population is 26,355,000. It is the most polluted country in the world, with barely 10% of its original forest cover remaining. Driving is on the left lane, its citizens take off their shoes when entering the home, most don't drink alcohol, and don't smile often, as in their culture, smiling can be interpreted as a sign of immaturity.

Although it is a small country (similar to Suriname or Uruguay), its population exceeds that of Mexico or Russia, with more than 175.6 million people (projected to 2025). It is one of the most densely populated countries on the planet, with 1,355 inhabitants per square kilometer.

Its economy, barely larger than that of Venezuela or Haiti, depends primarily on the textile industry (more than 90% of its exports), agriculture, construction, shipbreaking, finance, and tourism. However, wages are very low.

Bangladesh has been unable to make progress due to a combination of factors:

- Military governments

- Natural disasters
- Global warming
- Corruption
- Anti-democratic policies
- Limited press freedom
- Difficulty doing business

Still, there are leaders fighting to change this situation. According to the IOM, 8% of Bangladeshis have emigrated to countries such as Saudi Arabia, Malaysia, the United Arab Emirates, and the United Kingdom, bringing the total number of Bangladeshis expected to reach more than 14 million by 2024.

New York: The city everyone wants to reach

New York is considered the capital of the world due to its financial, cultural, artistic, commercial, and diplomatic influence. It is home to institutions such as the Stock Exchange, the UN, and numerous multinational corporations. It is a global hub of opportunity that welcomes people from all corners of the globe.

It has one of the most diverse migrant populations in the world. From the 19th century, when European immigration began, until today, it has been a welcoming place for millions. Established communities serve as a support network for new immigrants.

Hispanics, primarily from the Dominican Republic, Mexico, Ecuador, Venezuela, and Colombia, have arrived in large waves, many from Texas and Arizona. New York has been known for making life easier for migrants. However, with political changes, the situation could change.

One of the most complicated issues remains housing due to its high cost. Shelter networks and assistance programs such as the immediate response cards (prepaid debit cards) with food subsidies offering up to $350 per week have been maintained, a program that ended with the new Trump administration.

Bangladesh: A country many want to leave

In contrast, Bangladesh is a country that expels migrants due to a lack of infrastructure, poverty, vulnerability to climate change, low-paying jobs, and political instability.

Social mobility is limited, and structural inequality prevents much of the population from improving their quality of life. Many Bangladeshis simply have no way to stay.

New York accepts migrants because it can pay. Bangladesh expels migrants because it has no way to retain them.

As long as the system continues to operate this way—unbalanced, unequal—airplanes, rafts, deserts, mountains, and illegal crossings
will continue to be escape routes from a global economy that has forgotten its balance.

Performance in the place of origin

The economic, social, and environmental conditions of the place of origin play a crucial role in people's decision to migrate. Generally speaking, migration is a response to the constraints and inequalities that communities face in their original environments.

Ultimately, humans and non-humans migrate due to the deterioration of their environment, although the responses vary according to the needs of each species.

In a semi-arid region of Mexico, a peasant family decides to abandon their home due to a lack of water. At the same time, the mountain goats that inhabited the nearby hills migrate to the other side of the mountain range in search of pasture. In their new location, the human migrants must learn to coexist with the wildlife that already lives there.

Better salaries at the destination

In a small town in southern Mexico, Jorge lived with his family working a corn field. Rainfall had been scarce in recent years, and the harvest no longer met their needs. Meanwhile, prices had fallen due to strong competition from large agricultural companies.

One day, Jorge overheard his neighbor talking about his cousin, who worked in the strawberry fields in California and Plant City, Florida, earning in a month what Jorge earned in a year.

The decision was difficult, but Jorge packed his few belongings and crossed the border into the United States, leaving his wife and two children behind. In his absence, the plot of land was abandoned, overrun by weeds and coyotes in search of food. While Jorge worked long hours in the strawberry fields, he dreamed of returning to his village with enough money to rebuild his life. However, in the village, his family faced a changing environment: nature was reclaiming what humans had left behind.

Jorge's story illustrates how economic factors, especially the pursuit of better wages, not only drive human migration but also trigger movements in non-human ecosystems.

The search for better wages is a key cause of human migration, reflecting the desire to improve the quality of life, overcome poverty, and provide opportunities for future generations. Similarly, in non-human migration, the search for resources and better living conditions is equally essential, drawing a fascinating parallel between the two worlds. Both processes are driven by the need to adapt and survive in a changing environment.

Poverty and lack of opportunities

Pedro, a man who left his homeland due to extreme poverty, finds refuge in a garbage dump in a foreign country. There, he meets a pack of dogs who, initially fearful, begin to approach him, attracted by his constant presence.

Over time, Pedro bonds with them, recognizing that the struggle for survival is a shared one. On cold nights, the dogs curl up beside him, providing warmth. During the day, the animals become his allies, warning him of danger and pointing out garbage piles where there is something useful or saleable. Despite his own poverty, Pedro feeds them some of the little he collects.

This story shows how, in contexts of poverty and migration, networks of solidarity are woven that ignore species, demonstrating that the struggle for survival can unite living beings across all differences.

Poverty and lack of opportunities emerge as one of the main causes driving people to leave their countries of origin in search of a better future. These structural conditions of inequality generate a cycle of social exclusion that forces people to migrate, often facing extreme danger and hardship.

Emotional contagion and collective migration

When we talk about seeking opportunities, we could say that humans also act through emotional contagion and empathy. This is explained by the German philosopher and psychologist Theodor Lipps, known for his studies in this area. His theory of emotional contagion is based on how the emotions and mental states of an individual or group can be transmitted to others without direct verbal communication, simply through observation and imitation.

This means that when a community faces economic hardship, insecurity, or lack of opportunity, discontent and frustration spread among its members, spurring a search for change.

When some people emigrate and share their experiences with those still in their countries of origin, an emotional contagion is generated that reinforces the idea that migration is a viable solution. This can lead to a mass exodus, where more people decide to leave, not only for economic or political reasons, but also due to the emotional influence of those who have already migrated.

Nowadays, social media and the media also contribute to this emotional contagion. They do so by showing historical images and photos of the best tourist spots that family members post online on weekends when they have their "off" days. These images, along with the stories of migrants who have improved their lives in other countries, can generate a collective desire for mobility, driven by the perception—sometimes idealized—that abroad offers a better quality of life.

Forced migration

"They can cut all the flowers, but they can't stop the spring."

—Pablo Neruda

Several causes of forced migration can be enumerated, such as armed conflict and violence, natural disasters, climate change, lack of basic resources, and even development projects themselves, which often force entire communities to relocate.

We take the case of the construction of the Three Gorges Dam in China, which displaced more than 1.3 million people. Construction began in 1994 and was completed in 2006, although the reservoir reached its maximum capacity in 2010. It was one of the largest and most controversial infrastructure projects in the world due to its environmental, social, and cultural impacts. Hundreds of towns and cities were flooded, and a large amount of cultural heritage was lost.

Another clear example of forced migration is the case of Venezuela, which since the late 2010s has experienced one of the largest mass exoduses in Latin America and the world. More than 8 million people have left the country due to hyperinflation, insecurity, food and medicine shortages, and political repression.

Migrants, unable to take their pets with them, often leave them behind. However, some people choose to migrate with their animals, facing great difficulties in providing for them. Here we clearly see the symbiosis between humans and nonhumans, and how forcibly displaced people not only cope with the loss of their homes but also seek to preserve their bonds with their pets and nature.

José Alejandro Rodríguez Peñaranda, a 12-year-old boy from the Ábrego region of Norte de Santander, Colombia, performed on a singing and talent show in Colombia, accompanied by his guitar. He left a powerful message in his song:

"That's what you hear about Catatumbo, that there's a lot of violence, but today I'm not here to talk about the ugliness of Catatumbo, but rather about the beauty of this land. Catatumbo is art, Catatumbo is culture, Catatumbo is music. As a leader, I want to tell all children that anyone who picks up an instrument will never think of picking up a weapon."

There's a region in Colombia that's increasingly being hit by violence, known as the "region of eternal thunder": Catatumbo, located in the department of Norte de Santander. Until recently, it was the largest cocaine-producing area in the world, with more than 50,000 hectares under cultivation, according to data from current President Gustavo Petro.

This region maintains the presence of illegal armed groups, including the ELN (National Liberation Army), FARC dissidents, paramilitary groups, drug cartels, and the Tren de Aragua, a Venezuelan criminal group with a presence throughout Latin America, Europe, and the United States.

These criminal gangs fight for territorial power, and coca leaf cultivation is the main source of fuel for the armed conflict.

The historical absence of the State has left communities vulnerable to the control of illegal actors, exacerbating poverty, exclusion, and the lack of basic services. Many families have abandoned their farms—oil palm, cassava, and livestock—to migrate to nearby cities such as Cúcuta, Bucaramanga, and others, increasing both internal and external migration flows.

Search for a better quality of life

Migration in search of a better quality of life is another important reason that drives people to leave their places of origin.

This cause can be analyzed from various disciplines such as economics, sociology, psychology, and biology. By including the symbiosis between humans and nonhumans, the analysis is enriched by highlighting the interactions and mutual dependencies between people and their environment, including other living beings.

Quality of life is a multidimensional concept that encompasses aspects such as access to healthcare, education, housing, employment, and security. People migrate when they feel their current environment lacks opportunities for advancement, and they seek out territories where these factors are more accessible.

From another perspective, Frans de Waal, in his book *The Age of Empathy* , explains how humans can become as competitive as non-humans. For example, chimpanzees have made progress in conflict resolution and collaboration: to avoid disputes, they kiss and hug each other after fighting. They compete for food, sexual partners, and territory.

De Waal observes that primates spend about 10% of their daily work maintaining social bonds. How much time do we humans spend rebuilding our own?

We humans can be described as highly competitive, collaborative animals, with a great capacity for tolerance and involvement. This makes us masters of connection, and social bonds themselves restrict competition. When we need each other, we support each other. We are social gregarious, which allows us to show solidarity with others when the common ground is survival and the pursuit of a better quality of life… while also being selfish to some degree.

Combining many of the decisions made by both humans and non-humans, we can say that we are always seeking better living conditions. We often act out of herd instinct.

A clear example: the mass migration to the United States over the past four years, where many families arrived with their pets, dogs and cats, not exactly to eat them, but as an essential part of their family. With substantial changes until January 20, 2025, which you already know about.

We humans tend to imitate what others do. Many people migrate, influenced by group synergy or simply by a collective emotional outpouring that unites us in the desire for a better life.

When family members, friends, or neighbors begin to see migration as an opportunity, others follow their example. We undertake actions in sync with those with whom we identify and belong.

Trip to the United States along the Darien Route

This route, widely used by a variety of nationalities, was initially traveled primarily by Haitians and Cubans seeking to reach the United States. However, in recent years—until January 2025—its composition has changed significantly. Today, it is traveled by South Americans, Caribbeans, Africans, and Asians.

Of the South American group, the most present have been Venezuelans, who, as a result of the economic and political crisis in their country, began to migrate, many after having lived in Colombia, Peru, Ecuador, or Chile.

Another important group is Ecuadorians, who have begun to take this route more aggressively since Mexico introduced visa requirements in 2021. Colombians, despite historically being a receiving country, have also used the Darien Route, especially those fleeing violence, poverty, or seeking better opportunities and a better quality of life.

Peruvians and Bolivians have also joined, motivated by economic crises and a lack of jobs. Central Americans—Hondurans, Salvadorans, Nicaraguans, and Guatemalans—have also used this route, especially when their journey to the United States begins in the south of the continent.

As for people from Africa and Asia, many migrants from West Africa (Senegal, Ghana, Cameroon) and Asia (Bangladesh, India, Nepal) arrive in Brazil or Ecuador, taking advantage of the ease of obtaining visas, and from there they cross the Darien jungle to continue their journey to the United States.

The adventure begins: the Darien jungle

Entire families travel this dangerous route that connects Colombia to Panama. The Darien jungle is one of the most inhospitable and dangerous regions on the continent.

The journey begins in Colombia. Migrants arrive from the Necoclí or Turbo region in the department of Antioquia, and from there take boats to Capurganá or Acandí, on the Chocó coast, very close to the border with Panama.

From Capurganá or Acandí, they begin their trek on foot through the Darién jungle. This is the most dangerous part of the route. The hike can last between five and ten days, depending on weather conditions. Along the way, they face swollen rivers, mountainous terrain, wild animals, disease, and armed groups.

After crossing the jungle, the migrants arrive at the indigenous village of Bajo Chiquito, the first checkpoint in Panama. From there, they travel by canoe along the river to Metetí, where they are taken to migratory stations.

Road to Central America

Once in Panama, migrants continue toward Costa Rica, crossing through the Paso Canoas border post. They then travel through Nicaragua, usually by clandestine transport, as the Nicaraguan government does not allow migrant transit.

In Honduras, they must register at an immigration office before continuing on to Guatemala. From there, they cross into Mexico via the Suchiate River, on the border with Tapachula, Chiapas.

Once in Mexico, migrants are trying to reach the U.S. border, using buses, trains like La Bestia, or on foot.

Currently, we can say that three main routes are used in Mexico:

- To Reynosa or Matamoros (to cross into Texas),
- Towards Ciudad Juárez (to cross to El Paso),
- Towards Tijuana (to cross into California).

Crossing into the US: Before and After 2025

Until January 20, 2025, under other immigration policies, migrants attempted to cross through the desert or the Rio Grande. Another option was to surrender at a port of entry to request asylum, or to pay coyotes or traffickers, although this carried high risks: fraud, kidnapping, and uncared-for deaths.

In our investigation, we spoke with many people from different countries, each with their own unique story. Some paid coyotes, local authorities, or criminal gangs that control the migration business at the borders between countries. The cost per person is estimated to have ranged between $3,000 and $5,000.

Others, with a more business-minded mindset—not to call them white slavers—created fake "tourism agencies" from their countries of origin, charging large sums of money. They organized trips, housed their clients in hotels in Mexico, and prepared them to be received by coyotes. A well-synchronized macro-business, with the complicity of some authorities.

This business turned some into millionaires, others into victims, and many more into names lost in oblivion.

Data and reality

According to data from international organizations such as the IOM and UNHCR, which analyze trends and risks, it is estimated that, in the last four years up to 2024, and part of the data available from February and March 2025, around 1,206,000 people entered the Darien Route. That is, people who managed to reach Panama. However, not all of them reached their final destination in the United States.

In the first quarter of 2025, there were only 408 entries of people into the US, a 99% decrease, attributed to a combination of strict policies (Trump administration since January 2025)

.

Social causes

Socially driven human migration is a complex phenomenon that responds to a combination of individual, family, cultural, and community dynamics that drive people to leave their homes. These dynamics not only force people to migrate, but also influence narratives and policies that dehumanize migrants in receiving countries.

It is also important to highlight how these dynamics affect the symbiosis between humans and their non-human environment, since when the social fabric in the regions of origin breaks down, so does the connection with the environment.

In non-humans, migration may be due to seasonal changes, availability of food resources, alterations in ecosystems, reproductive cycles, climate changes, or predatory pressure.

Family reunification

The family is the fundamental foundation of society. The nuclear family is the group composed of parents and children; it is the basic core of coexistence and upbringing in most societies. It can be:

- Biparental, when both parents are present,
- Single parent, when only one parent is present,
- Homoparental, formed by a same-sex couple and their children,
- Reconstituted nuclear, resulting from the union of two people who contribute children from previous relationships.

These models reflect the adaptation of the family structure to the social, economic, and cultural changes of the 21st century. Factors such as the increase in divorce, remarriage, acceptance of same-sex relationships, and assisted reproductive technologies have contributed to this diversification.

However, there are indigenous cultures with other family models, such as the life of the inhabitants of Namibia, a country located in southwest Africa whose capital is Windhoek. This country is known for its arid geography, which includes the Namib Desert, one of the oldest in the world. There, the family generally presents traditional roles with very specific cultural traits.

In many communities, men are seen as providers and women as caretakers of the home and family. Children are not raised exclusively by their biological parents, but by the entire community. Uncles, aunts, and grandparents play a key role in their education and development.

The Himba, an indigenous community inhabiting northern Namibia, have a social structure, including a polygynous one. It is common for men to have more than one wife. Each wife has her own hut and space within the settlement. Furthermore, the Himba share their wives with close friends and visitors as a sign of trust, hospitality, and respect. Everything is done with consideration and consent of both parties: the man makes the offer, but the woman approves or disapproves.

This strengthens community ties, empowerment, and female autonomy. Women are the backbone of community life. They transmit knowledge, manage household resources, and work as a team. Education in these communities is an open and participatory system: children learn by observing and helping, which fosters their connection to culture and tradition. Co-parenting ensures that all adults care about the well-being of the children, thus creating a support network that transcends the nuclear family.

From another perspective, Frans de Waal describes how, for primates, the family unit is fundamental—very similar to human behavior. In one of his observations, he recounts how an anthropoid mother, upon noticing that her offspring cannot cross between trees, returns, shakes her tree until it leans toward the other, creating a natural bridge with her body. In this way, she allows her offspring to cross. This situation goes beyond coordination: it is about family problem-solving and a deep emotional connection within the group.

Family reunification is also a major cause of migration, both among humans and non-humans (in the animal kingdom). In both cases, this motivation responds to an emotional, biological, and social need to strengthen emotional bonds within a group.

In humans, the emotional and affective aspect prevails significantly: the need to be close to loved ones, especially after long periods of separation, is a powerful driver. This includes parents, children, partners, and extended family members.

The economic aspect is also a connector: many people migrate to join relatives who have already settled in another region or country and enjoy better living conditions. This allows them to share resources and seek new opportunities.

From a legal perspective, many immigration policies include avenues for family reunification, such as specific visas for spouses, children, or dependents of residents or citizens.

However, family reunification is often hampered by legal and political barriers that complicate or delay the process. This generates feelings of anguish, stress, anxiety, and uncertainty in separated families, and triggers emotional stressors that we will later explore in the psychological consequences of migration.

Marriage (papers, social networks)

Marriage plays a central role as a social factor in migration. It can occur for love or for convenience, with the goal of settling in new lands and accessing rights and opportunities for legalizing immigration status. However, marriage of convenience, or for "papers," raises ethical and legal dilemmas. The line between a genuine relationship and a strategic transaction is blurred, and many countries have tightened controls to prevent fraudulent unions.

Today, digital platforms play a crucial role in the formation of these marriages. Social media and dating apps have changed the way people meet, crossing borders. Some platforms include:

- Tinder, Bumble, and Badoo: Although designed for romantic encounters, some people use them to find partners with citizenship in countries where they want to migrate.
- Facebook and migrant groups: There are Facebook communities where migrants share information about legal procedures, and some post searches for couples willing to marry for "papers."
- Reddit and Telegram forums: In these spaces, users ask about experiences with marriages of convenience and seek advice on the risks and benefits. In these environments, some people seek a partner with citizenship in the destination country, while others, already residents, offer marriage in exchange for money or mutual agreements.

Given the rise in marriages of convenience worldwide, many countries have implemented stricter measures to detect marriage fraud, making these practices riskier. Authorities have developed strategies to verify their authenticity, such as the following:

1. Separate interviews with couples: In countries like the U.S. and Canada, authorities conduct interviews to assess whether the relationship is genuine, asking detailed questions about the couple's life, such as:
   o When and how did you meet?
   o Where was your first date?
   o Where and when did they get married?
   o Where did you spend your honeymoon (if there was one)?
   o Who pays the rent or mortgage?
   o How do you divide the expenses?
   o Who wakes up first in the morning?
   o Who prepares breakfast?
   o What time do you usually get home from work?
   o How do you spend your free time together?

   Questions are also asked about family and friends, intimacy, personal routines, recent events, and future plans.

2. Social Media Monitoring: Some immigration agencies review the social media activity of green card applicants to verify whether they are actually in a romantic relationship.
3. Cohabitation Investigations: In some cases, immigration officers may make unannounced visits to the couple's home to verify whether they are living together. If fraud is detected, penalties such as fines, deportation, reentry bans, criminal records, and even imprisonment may apply.
4. Requests for proof of a genuine relationship: Joint bank accounts, housing bills in both names, photographs from different times and places, validation of food preferences, location of each other's clothing, among others, may be required.

In the case of the United States, the current Trump administration has seen major changes in this regard, implementing policies that have tightened certain aspects of the immigration process. Scrutiny during interviews and the review of documents to detect possible marriage fraud have been increased.

However, marriage to a U.S. citizen remains a legal path for a foreign spouse to obtain permanent residency in the United States. This right is protected by the Immigration and Nationality Act (INA) and cannot be eliminated solely by executive order. Any change would require an act of Congress. Furthermore, it is a fundamental right recognized in the U.S. Constitution.

The Fourteenth Amendment to the Constitution, ratified in 1868, contains the clause known as the Citizenship Clause, which establishes that all persons born or naturalized in the United States are citizens of the country and of the state in which they reside.

The relevant text reads as follows:

"All persons born or naturalized in the United States, and subject to its jurisdiction, are citizens of the United States and of the State wherein they reside."

Family-based immigration is one of the main avenues for legal residency, for obtaining a Green Card (permanent residency).

There is another option for investors who can bring their families to the U.S.: the "gold card," a recent proposal by President Trump. Applicants must make a one-time payment of $5 million to the government to be eligible.

This initiative aims to attract high-net-worth individuals, wealthy, world-class citizens who can contribute significantly to the U.S. economy, generating revenue that could be used to reduce the national deficit.

As an additional benefit, the program includes job creation and tax relief. It will be available to both individuals and companies wishing to invest in the country's economy.

Discrimination

Mateo was born in Paris, but his last name, Rahman, gave him away. His parents were Bangladeshi immigrants who came to France seeking a better future. After graduating with honors in engineering, Mateo soon discovered that his last name carried more weight than his talent. At every job interview, he received strained smiles and evasive answers. Some companies wouldn't even call him, even though his resume was impeccable. A French friend, with lower qualifications than his, got the job at a prestigious technology firm, while Mateo was told his profile didn't fit the company's "culture." After years of fighting against an invisible barrier, Mateo made a difficult decision: to emigrate to Canada. There, in less than six months, he landed a position commensurate with his experience, without anyone questioning his last name or his origins. Years later, as he watched the snow fall from his office window in Toronto, he thought about his childhood. He remembered his parents, his family, his school, and the country where he was born and raised. He thought about Paris and everything he'd left behind. He hadn't left because he wanted to, but because his own country had made him feel like a foreigner.

Like Mateo, many of us who have left our countries of origin have experienced discrimination at some point: in direct contact with natives, with human crocodiles who have already settled, with other migrants from other countries, also in jobs, and with the authorities themselves.

The "Moroni Law" – Italy

Italy was one of the first countries to include migration as a crime in its penal code. Others subsequently followed suit. The Moroni Law is a set of measures on migration and public security, implemented during Roberto Moroni's term as Minister of the Interior in 2008. These provisions, approved in 2009, introduced significant changes to Italian migration legislation.

Among the main measures, the following stand out:

- Criminalization of illegal immigration: Illegal entry and residence in Italy became offenses punishable by fines of up to 10,000 euros.
- The law limited undocumented immigrants' access to basic services and social rights, such as housing.
- This created greater vulnerability, leaving people exposed to extreme conditions: living on the streets, lack of medical care, inadequate nutrition, and risk of substance abuse.
- According to studies, life expectancy in these conditions can be 20 to 30 years less than that of the general population.

Symbiosis and exclusion

Linking this situation to the symbiosis between humans and non-humans, we can establish an analogy with symbiotic relationships in nature: when policies criminalize and discriminate against migration, dynamics closer to parasitism are generated, where one party benefits at the expense of the other. Instead of harmonious coexistence, tensions and conflicts are fueled.

Current discrimination is part of a complex web of cultural, historical, and social prejudices that immigrants face, especially when their humanity and customs are derogatorily questioned. In many cases, immigrants are blamed for economic problems, crime, or pressure on social resources.

This narrative becomes a political tool to polarize society and, in some cases, to distract attention from the real problems facing governments.

Phrases like:

- *"Immigrants take our jobs"*
- *"Immigrants eat our dogs, our cats, our pets,"*
- *"They are a threat to our culture"*

reflect modern forms of discrimination amplified by social media and the media.

It's crucial to emphasize that immigrants bring not only customs and traditions, but also stories of success, professionalism, hard work, self-improvement, and valuable contributions to the communities where we arrive.

Because:
"Immigrants don't eat dogs or cats."

Search for better services (health – education)

The search for better services, such as education and healthcare, is another key factor driving migration.

Throughout history, people have left their regions or countries of origin in search of better living conditions for themselves and their families. In fact, many of us have achieved this, either through our own experience or that of close people—family members, friends—who have had great success stories.

And that, ultimately, is what the vast majority of us who migrate seek: to achieve what we call here the migratory ecstasy.

All these phenomena - as we have been reviewing - apply to both internal migrations (from the countryside to the city), as well as international migrations (from developing countries to countries with greater resources), and even to the emerging and visionary migration space to other planets, such as Mars, the red planet, insistently proposed by Elon Musk.

For those of us who have already experienced the first two types of migration, we will surely be delighted to experience the third: being part of a new human civilization, although it may not be enough if it does not generate real and profound changes.

Changes that will not come from external structures, but from within each individual.

Later, in Part III, we will share this vision from a futuristic perspective: the ecstasy of migration.

1. Health

"What affects health the most is poverty, which people experience unfairly."

Access to quality healthcare systems is one of the main reasons why many people migrate. In countries with weak healthcare systems, high costs, lack of medical infrastructure, shortage of professionals, inaccessibility to specialized treatments, and resource hogging in the value chain are part of the problem.

Often, we see that the same state entities or those that administer health care are responsible for disrupting the process, acquiring low-quality primary medicines that doctors prescribe so that the less fortunate can claim them at dispensaries.

We can't blame these professionals entirely. These organizations simply set a profit ceiling per person. If the doctor wants to help—out of his Hippocratic oath to preserve life, or out of human compassion—what he does is provide a private prescription, so the patient can purchase the medication on his own.

But a salaried person, earning a minimum wage, set by governments with public administration based on falsified indicators, is unable to afford to buy his medicines month after month, especially if they are expensive. So, he ends up rejoicing in the house of God, at His holy will, praying for his health, because he doesn't have enough money.

In fact, we know many intermediaries in the healthcare business who are millionaires in our countries. They are involved with the current political class to administer healthcare, generating handouts for their administrators, but carrying many deaths on their shoulders. That should weigh on their conscience—if they have any human conscience left. As someone close to this investigation said: *"That's the least of their concerns."*

As we've said throughout this study, we're not political critics, but we do want these analyses to serve as a catalyst for reflection on what degrades human beings from different perspectives, leading them to migrate. In this case, for health reasons.

Some examples of why people migrate for these reasons:

- Patients with chronic or rare diseases who require treatments not available in their country of origin.
- Families who migrate so that their children receive specialized medical care.
- Healthcare professionals who migrate in search of better job opportunities and access to advanced medical technology.

Emblematic cases include the migration of people from Latin America to the United States in search of medical care, as well as medical tourism in countries such as Canada, Germany, and Spain, where access to public health care is more equitable.

2. Education

"Education is the most powerful weapon which you can use to change the world."
—Nelson Mandela

Migration for educational reasons has been a constant throughout human history. We can look at several contexts:

At the university level, there are limitations, a lack of investment in educational quality, and insufficient infrastructure. Education has become a business, expensive and inaccessible to many sectors. Furthermore, governments prioritize defense issues, the arms race, and competitiveness.

New professionals, unable to find work in their home countries, migrate in search of employment opportunities across borders. When they decide not to return, the phenomenon of brain drain occurs: highly qualified professionals leave for another country in search of better conditions.

This process particularly affects developing countries, which are losing key talent in technology, science, health, and education.

A personal case: at the university where I completed my graduate studies in Colombia, the rector established agreements with a university in Spain. Professors were sent to train, but most never returned. Despite contractual clauses with penalties, the euro-peso conversion rate was so uneven that many preferred to pay and remain in the mother country.

From an evolutionary and symbiotic perspective, the desire to learn has evolved in both species. Primates have improved their tool use, both in captivity and in the wild.
For example:

- Chimpanzees crack nuts with stones, showing understanding of impact physics.
- They make sharp "spears" with their teeth to hunt small animals.
- Bonobos use sticks to measure the depth of the water.
- Orangutans use leaves as umbrellas or gloves.

In cities like Lopburi, Thailand—the "city of monkeys"—macaques steal glasses, cameras, food, and even attempt to steal babies. To recover stolen items, they trade food, demonstrating a high level of social learning.

When Albert Einstein was asked what the Third World War would be like, he replied:

"I don't know. But the fourth will be fought with sticks and stones."

Two possible interpretations:

1. Humanity will self-destruct in a nuclear war and we will return to the primitive age.

2. Our closest cousins will evolve so much that they will confront us.

Education is a determining factor in the decision to migrate. People seek academic opportunities for themselves or their children because education is seen as a means of social mobility and quality of life.

Frequent motivations:

- Access to prestigious universities and graduate programs.
- Schools with better infrastructure.
- Countries that offer free or accessible education.
- Innovative or specialized educational models.

An example is the migration of families to Finland or Germany, where public education is free and of high quality.

From our perspective, education and health are fundamental human rights. Their pursuit depends largely on how migration policies facilitate or hinder access.

Education is not only a factor in migration, but also a bridge between societies, a channel for integration, and a way to generate symbiotic relationships between migrants and host countries.

In indigenous communities, young people migrate to study and return to apply their knowledge to environmental protection , combining science and ancestral knowledge. This exchange benefits the human community and local ecosystems.

In non-humans, many species migrate to learn how to survive. Human education is not so different: we migrate in search of knowledge and the conditions to develop our skills.

- Humpback whales transmit songs and migratory routes to their calves as a form of education.
- Many species learn by imitation and experimentation, like humans.

Just as animals learn collectively, humans migrate to learn from the best educational systems and apply that knowledge in new environments.

Following Frans de Waal's thesis, migration for education is a manifestation of our cooperative and empathetic nature. Like many social species, learning is transmitted and generates symbiotic relationships that benefit both the individual and the community.

The pursuit of education reflects a deep instinct for cooperation and shared evolution, as we also see in chimpanzees, elephants, and bonobos.

This reinforces the idea that migration is a natural phenomenon, driven by the need to learn, adapt, and progress as a species.

Political causes (persecution - conflicts)

No political party, no voice, no leader can be stronger than oneself. Human beings must maintain their own personal autonomy under all circumstances. Differences of thought make us indivisible, with unparalleled rights such as equality and freedom.

Wars and conflicts.

Tell me, why don't people smile? Why are there weapons in their hands? Why are the men badly wounded? Tell me, tell me, why are the children abused? Why are the old forgotten? Why are the dreams forbidden? Tell me, tell me, God, I want to know. Tell me why you refuse to listen. There's still someone who might pray. Tell me, God, I want to know where all the truth lies. There's still someone who might know. Tell me... why don't the ice ridges cry anymore? Why don't the rivers sing anymore? Why have you left us alone? Tell me...

Author: José Luis Perales

it's part of our history, so much so that it has helped, at times, both advance and stop us. This applies to humans and non-humans alike.

Society itself has created forms of association that regularize the transition to this level: war. But the syndrome we carry within us can take over: the desire for ambition, competition, cruelty, lack of ethics, solidarity, and values, often more than we can handle. With all the filters we've gone through as humanity—two world wars and the third on the verge of breaking out—it's been difficult to remove these feelings from our being. We've struggled internally with this immeasurable force that surpasses our control: power, hatred, selfishness, envy, the new global expansionism, the new colonizers... We've already been through that, for God's sake!

There were other ancestors of ours who achieved freedom with homemade weapons, spears, swords, and hand-to-hand combat. We managed to free ourselves, as in our American continent. But our new legislators want to establish this new model of warfare—or not a new one at that—something that had already been overcome in the evolutionary process of society. This motive for war had been left behind. In the 21st century, we are resuming it. Surely Hitler himself exemplified this with the European invasion: it proved that power is not enough to achieve his goals. Always arriving at the same thing: War – destruction.

The irony is that, although we've evolved for millions of years—from those early hominids who walked upright in Africa to this "modern" human being who today browses social media and flies—in that process, we could say we've achieved the basics, the essentials, to survive. Some with fewer possibilities than others, but we have them. We just have to work for them.

So why should we kill each other? Why do we have to resolve disagreements with violence? We see it every day on the news: wars that displace thousands of people, forced migrations, territorial conflicts, political polarization that turns into hatred and aggression.

Can we all ask ourselves: Have we really made progress?
How are we different from that species that once fought with spears to defend a river?

With drones aimed at key points—like those being used in the war between Ukraine and Russia today, as you read this—how many young people are dying there? Our brilliant minds of the future... how many? Every young person who dies is one less plan realized. They've killed each other so much that they're using paid mercenary soldiers whose only interest is killing the other side. They don't take into account the causes of the war itself; in fact, they don't even know.

From another perspective, according to studies conducted by primatologist and scientist Frans de Waal, human beings are, at their core, violent and amoral. We have an uncontrollable aggressive impulse that finds an outlet in war. Although we are not the only primates capable of killing our fellow humans, we are capable of controlling our fighting instinct.

Also presenting is Konrad Lorenz, winner of the Nobel Prize in 1973 for his pioneering studies of animal behavior in their natural environment. His research has had a profound impact on how we understand the behavior of both animals and humans. By highlighting the instinctual bases of behavior, he analyzed how instinctual patterns influence animal and human life. Lorenz was a great proponent of the idea that aggression is in our genes. This murderous attitude became humanity's Mark of Cain.

There is one weapon, perhaps one of the most important, to protect ourselves from war—for both humans and non-humans: it's called compassion and empathy. The new generation of humanity must be based on these foundations: respect for others, where diversity of thought is respected. Let us achieve unrestricted freedom. We will look at this thesis in more detail later.

The global political class is prepared to spread narratives based on the level of influence it can exert on people, always seeking to benefit the power circles in most of its proposals. One thing we, as a modern society, cannot do is view politicians as pharaohs, kings, or emperors.

Let's review a narrative that can help us understand this type of collective emotionalism:

The Pharaoh's Curse is a legend that arose following the discovery of Tutankhamun's tomb in 1922 by British archaeologist Howard Carter and his team. According to the myth, anyone who disturbed the Pharaoh's rest would be punished with death or terrible misfortune. Shortly after, people involved in the excavation suffered unexpected deaths or mysterious illnesses. One such case was the death of Lord Carnarvon, sponsor of the expedition. It was later learned that Carnarvon died in March 1923 from a blood infection caused by a mosquito bite. The media did their sensational work very well: they attributed his death to the Pharaoh's Curse. This myth was used to generate mystery and fear toward those who dared to interfere with the Pharaoh's rest.

We can associate the curse of Pharaoh Tutankhamun with the central theme of this book in the political phrase:

"Immigrants eat our dogs and cats."

…through the idea of how myths, prejudices, and narratives influence people's perceptions and behaviors. Both concepts revolve around power and persuasion. The phrase is an exaggerated narrative that generates distrust, rejection, and fear toward those of us who take the risk—or the need—to migrate and leave our countries.

These narratives show us that they are powerful tools, used for political or social purposes to control public perception, justify discriminatory policies, and foster prejudice against immigrants.

By demystifying both narratives, we discover the richness of what they truly represent: the pharaohs and their cultural legacy connect us to the greatness of human civilization. "Immigrants don't eat dogs or cats" connects us to the possibilities of a global society, rich in diversity, empathy, and cooperation.

Political persecution

Of the causes we've examined, one in particular is political persecution. A strong reason is fear: when fear takes over everyday life, when words can cost you your freedom or your life, there's no choice but to flee.

Political persecution has forced millions of people to leave their countries, from Venezuelan refugees escaping the crisis to Cuban exiles in Miami. History is full of stories of those who had to leave everything behind to save themselves. In many cases, we are not criminals, as demonstrated by the mass deportations currently taking place under anti-immigration policies like the one we are experiencing in the United States. This has led to diplomatic ruptures between countries, such as what happened with the first two planes returned by Colombian President Gustavo Petro. This action came after a diplomatic dispute between Colombia and the United States.

Initially, President Petro rejected the arrival of US flights carrying deportees, arguing that they could not treat Colombian migrants as criminals. In response, President Donald Trump threatened to impose tariffs on Colombian products. Eventually, an agreement was reached in which Colombia agreed to receive the first 205 deportees on January 28, 2025, using its own military aircraft, guaranteeing a dignified return for its citizens.

Government instability

Government instability is one of the main causes of migration in many parts of the world. Corrupt governments, civil wars, coups d'état, human rights violations, and a lack of economic opportunities create unsustainable living conditions for millions of people, forcing them to seek safety and stability in other countries.

Joseba Achotegui explains that those who flee for political reasons leave behind not only their homes, but also their identity, their support networks, and the sense of security their home country provided. This grief is compounded when the destination country perceives them as a burden or a threat, rather than recognizing their suffering and resilience.

Environmental causes

Environmental factors have been decisive in the history of humanity and its mobility. Climate change, desertification, rising sea levels, and natural disasters have forced populations to move in search of better living conditions. However, this migration is not only a survival response, but also a reflection of the symbiotic relationship between humans and their environment. This migration is also part of a natural process, but also a consequence of how we have affected ecosystems.

Global warming

Global warming is the sustained increase in the planet's average temperature, primarily due to the accumulation of greenhouse gases (GHGs) in the atmosphere. These gases, such as carbon dioxide (CO_2) and methane (CH_4), come mostly from the burning of fossil fuels—primarily gasoline and diesel—deforestation, and industrial activities.

Global warming affects human and non-human migration because it alters the climatic and environmental conditions that allow life in certain territories. As the planet warms, ecosystems change, and many species—including humans—are forced to move in search of better survival conditions. In the case of animals, their plight is worsening because their habitats are disappearing and they have nowhere else to move.

Paris Agreement on climate change

The Paris Agreement on climate change was adopted on December 12, 2015, during the United Nations Climate Change Conference (COP21) in Paris, France. One hundred and ninety-five countries and the European Union signed the agreement, committing to reducing greenhouse gas emissions and limiting global warming to well below 2 degrees Celsius above pre-industrial levels, with efforts to limit warming to no more than 1.5 degrees Celsius.

All UN member states participated and signed the agreement in 2016, with the exception of Eritrea, Iran, Iraq, Libya, South Sudan, and Yemen, which did not ratify it immediately.

The United States signed the agreement under the Barack Obama administration, but in 2017, during Donald Trump's first administration, it announced its withdrawal, which became effective in 2020. However, in 2021, President Joe Biden rejoined the agreement. Now, in his second term, President Donald Trump signed an executive order on January 20, 2025, to once again withdraw the United States from the Paris Agreement. The withdrawal has drawn criticism both domestically and internationally, as it could weaken global efforts to combat climate change and undermine the United States' credibility in future environmental negotiations.

Key commitments of the Paris Agreement

1. Reduce greenhouse gas emissions to achieve carbon neutrality in the second half of the 21st century.
2. Submit climate action plans (NDCs) every five years. Each country defines its own goals and actions based on its national capabilities and circumstances, with increasingly ambitious emission reduction targets.

   Examples of NDCs in some countries:

   o The United States has pledged to reduce its emissions by 50–52% by 2030 compared to 2005 levels.
   o China has pledged to reduce the carbon intensity of its GDP by more than 65% by 2030 compared to 2005 levels and achieve carbon neutrality by 2060.
   o The European Union seeks to reduce its emissions by at least 55% by 2030 compared to 1990.
3. Financially support developing countries, with a target of $100 billion annually to assist in climate change adaptation and mitigation.

4. Strengthen the resilience and adaptation of vulnerable countries to climate impacts.

Despite broad support, many countries have not fully met their commitments, and global warming continues to increase. At annual climate summits (COP), countries continue to negotiate new strategies to accelerate climate action.

Natural disasters

Natural disasters are one of the main manifestations of environmental factors that drive migration, both in humans and non-humans, as they abruptly and, in many cases, irreversibly alter the environment in which they live, forcing them to move in search of safety and stability.

From the perspective of symbiosis with the environment, natural disasters can be seen as signs of an imbalance in the relationship between humans and their environment.

Some disasters, such as floods and landslides, are exacerbated by human action (deforestation, unplanned urbanization, climate change). Disaster-induced forced migration disrupts communities and ways of life, forcing people to rebuild their relationship with nature in a new territory.

Non-humans have developed acute senses to detect changes in the environment before disasters occur, making them living signs of environmental imbalances. They exhibit unusual behaviors before earthquakes and tsunamis; in many cultures, cases have been documented in which birds, dogs, cats, elephants, and other animals change their behavior before an earthquake or tsunami. Some change their migratory patterns, that is, they alter their routes in response to climate change, which can serve as an early warning of environmental problems so that humans can take preventive measures.

A palpable scientific explanation for this behavior can be seen in dogs: they can perceive primary seismic waves (P), which travel faster than secondary waves (S), which cause the strong shaking we humans feel. Some studies suggest that dogs can also perceive underwater seismic vibrations or changes in air pressure before a large wave hits the shore.

During the 2024 Indian Ocean tsunami, there were numerous reports of dogs refusing to approach the beach hours before the disaster, trying to alert their owners by howling and running frantically. Most curiously, they ran for higher ground.

The dog and the science of longevity

The dog is considered man's best friend. It is the non-human pet most beloved by humans. San Francisco-based biotechnology company Loyal has made progress in developing an anti-aging pill intended to prolong the healthy lifespan of dogs. This drug, designed for canines 10 years of age or older and weighing at least 6 kg, has been approved by the U.S. Food and Drug Administration (FDA). However, confirmation of its safety and the ability to produce it on a large scale is currently awaited.

The Dog Aging Project, for example, is investigating the use of rapamycin, an immunosuppressant drug used in humans, with the goal of extending lifespan and improving cardiac and cognitive function in canines. These studies not only seek to benefit pets but could also provide valuable information for research on human longevity, given that dogs share similar environments and age-related conditions as people.

These research efforts are a reflection of the deep symbiotic bond between humans and non-humans, especially companion animals. Dogs have been with humans for thousands of years; they have migrated together and evolved not only physically but also in their social behavior to adapt to our needs and emotions. They are the ones who have had to learn to understand us.

Frans de Waal, in *The Age of Empathy* , highlights that humans are not the only ones capable of feeling complex emotions and that living with animals has strengthened our ability to empathize with them.

Climate change

Climate change has established itself as a determining environmental factor in contemporary migratory movements. Many phenomena, such as prolonged droughts, floods, and intense storms, deteriorate living conditions in various regions of the planet, forcing entire communities to move in search of safer environments and basic resources.

According to data from the International Organization for Migration (IOM), approximately 31.8 million new internal displacements were recorded in 2022 due to climate-related disasters, with floods and storms being the main causes.

From our perspective, it is crucial to recognize how climate change exacerbates humanitarian and migration crises. For example, Haiti has faced multiple natural disasters, such as earthquakes and hurricanes, which have devastated its infrastructure and economy. This, coupled with political instability and violence, has forced more than 500,000 people to flee their country since 2010, seeking refuge primarily in the United States.

Fortunately, their only destination is not just Springfield, Ohio, where it was claimed that Haitian immigrants were eating dogs and cats, generating outrage, intolerance, persecution, and general disrespect toward the migrant community in the United States.

One of our general causes and motives for this book is to show an antagonistic message, showing that: "Immigrants don't eat dogs or cats."

CHAPTER 5

The power between humans and non-humans

The symbiosis of power between humans and non-humans is closely related: we're all basically driven by the same thing: someone wants to get their hands on it. Evolutionary biologist Richard Dawkins argues that we are the only species on Earth that can rebel against the tyranny of selfish replicators. At the same time, Darwin believed that humanity is based on the social instincts we share with other animals.

Anthropomorphic apes (orangutans, gorillas, bonobos, and chimpanzees) tend to support winners in power sometimes and losers at other times. This relationship is based on studies of the social behavior of primates such as chimpanzees and bonobos. In these, power dynamics are strongly influenced by coalitions and political strategies. Chimpanzees, for example, establish hierarchies through alliances, and subordinate individuals often support dominant leaders who demonstrate strength and the ability to maintain stability in the group. This behavior is not unique to non-human primates; in human societies, many people are also observed to support successful leaders, reinforcing their power through social recognition and legitimation, not only in the political sphere but also in the corporate sphere.

In our opinion, one of the strongest drivers of migration is power, which significantly influences decision-making for both human and non-human mobility. Power, especially Machiavellian power—especially those who embrace his thesis "the end justifies the means"—is desired by those who want to climb the social ladder or simply want to stay there. We see how many leaders encapsulate power in ideological-political discourse, manipulating the masses, as the current Venezuelan president, Nicolás Maduro, and his elite do, with the intention of remaining in power, no matter the cost. An adverse human power is worth mentioning here for the damage it continues to cause today, with political maneuvers such as those carried out on July 28, 2024. The National Electoral Council declared Maduro elected with 51.20% of the votes, while opposition leader Edmundo González reportedly obtained 44.2%, results highly questioned by the opposition led by María Corina Machado and the international community. But questioning is not enough: Venezuelan society is vulnerable, mistreated, and controlled by the Cartel of the Suns.

The ruling party has distorted Simón Bolívar's legacy, continuing to spread this narrative based on the figure of the Liberator with the intention of tugging at the heartstrings of the Creole people who gave us freedom. This rhetoric makes it easier to subjugate them, adding prospects of prosperity, liberty, justice, unity, and human dignity. These are well-supported arguments that carry a subliminal message and psychological confinement that people have yet to decipher. But the time will come. Just as Venezuela officially liberated itself from Spanish rule on July 24, 1821, in the Battle of Carabobo, led by Bolívar, it is impossible that 200 years later someone will revisit that context as Chávez did on February 2, 1999, with the slogan of the "Bolivarian Revolution," with an emphasis on 21st-century socialism. Celebrating the Constitution, dressing up like the wolf in Little Red Riding Hood's tale: a wolf in grandmother's clothing, posing as a right-wing democrat, he eventually became the opposite: a right-wing dictator. His popular appeal was so strong that he even succeeded in changing the country's name to the Bolivarian Republic of Venezuela, in order to subjugate its people. However, he did not come in the name of the Spanish Crown, but rather out of his own interests, and from a community divergently aligned by the emotionalisms of power.

Non-human entities have processes similar to ours. There's also an internal power struggle. One member always seeks to dominate others, to subdue their pack, to be the leader in their own social structure. We'll examine these behaviors in our closest relatives, such as chimpanzees and bonobos.

Coalitions emerge among chimpanzees, which are key to seizing power. We know this: the same thing works in humans. In the chimpanzee community, no male can assert himself, at least not for long. The group has the authority to overthrow anyone. So the leader must prevent this situation; he must be very skilled at forming gangs and allies to strengthen his position. Maintaining power is a challenge: a balance must be maintained to keep allies happy and prevent the masses from rebelling.

Once established in power, one source that can cause or motivate the loss of power—or division within it—is sex, since alpha males enjoy extraordinary sexual privileges. They don't allow other males to approach their most desirable females, but this isn't always the case. There are exceptions, according to coalition negotiations. There are some close friends who have privileges. This type of pact can become dangerous over time. As they gain trust, they begin to interfere in other matters. Then things get ugly.

Brawls, even fights to the death, can occur, which can cause ruptures within these ruling coalitions and result in another male rising to power, becoming the alpha male. Power is the main driving force of the male chimpanzee. It is an aspiration that brings great satisfaction and benefits when achieved, and intense frustration when lost. There are some special manifestations of those who are waiting for their opportunity to rise, precisely when a situation like the one above occurs or when they play an important role as mediators, advisors, peacemakers, or powerful arbitrators who help resolve disputes. This special type of chimpanzee is very skilled. It becomes very popular with females, protects the less fortunate, and is effective in influencing the breakup of rival alliances through the "divide and conquer" tactic, which is very useful for both chimpanzees and humans, explains Frans de Waal in his book *The Ape Within U*.

Chimpanzee politics is like human politics: a set of individual and group strategies that clash to see which one prevails. There is a constant war between them and their communities. The injuries and stress caused by their constant power struggles lead to a high mortality rate.

This thesis of the symbiosis of human vs. non-human migration seeks to connect these two entities, how we resemble each other in our actions. Some of the decisions are similar, in some fragments of the quest for dominance. And when it's done in a distorted way, it affects us all, often forcing us to emigrate, even from our comfort zones, from our country, family, home, and entire lives—perhaps better established in some cases—than what we are exposed to.

In chimpanzees, when a stable hierarchy is established, pressures are eliminated and confrontation is reduced, as all subordinates avoid conflict. Everyone is better off: group members can move around confidently, groom each other, play, and calm their worries, because no one feels insecure. Now, if any of them tries to challenge the established order, the first thing to be abandoned is play. Now things get serious. A ritual among them is not only about power, it's also about harmony. The alpha male immediately assumes a haughty position, with his hair standing on end, to demonstrate who is the boss, who is in charge. Subordinates must prostrate themselves before him, kiss his hand, face, chest, or arms, bow their bodies, and look the alpha male up and down. That way, it's clear to them who is at the top.

Let's remember Iraqi dictator Saddam Hussein: Iraqi citizens were required to kiss his armpits as a sign of respect. Nicolás Maduro will soon reach such a horrendous position with the Venezuelan people. In any case, we humans have better defined these types of hierarchies—with a few exceptions. However, in large companies and military forces, chains of command often suppress democracy, especially when decisions need to be made on urgent matters.

Bonobos are another of our closest relatives. They have a unique social structure, where power is distributed in a particular way. Given their high sexual activity, males don't have much to worry about; the level of aggression is low. You could say they're less worried than their closest cousins, chimpanzees and humans. Female dominance predominates. Females tend to have more power and influence in groups. They form strong alliances with each other, can control resources, and make decisions about group movements.

In both anthropoids and humans, the female hierarchy is less contested. There is less rivalry, and that thirst for power is less pronounced. We see the case of women's influence in the family: they always gain the top position without having to fight. They gain the upper hand by having those maternal human skills: taking care of the home, the children, guiding homework, caring for pets. Women provide emotional balance in the home; they are the protective figure, and the older they get, the greater their influence.

There are special patterns among bonobos. Males tend to remain in their natal groups, while females migrate to other groups upon reaching maturity. These young females who migrate must earn their place in the group they join. They tactically form alliances with older females, employing social behaviors to gain acceptance, even engaging in homosexual relationships to integrate. As a benefit, this migration between groups helps prevent inbreeding, allows for genetic exchange between groups, and maintains population diversity.

Human communities, like the LGBTQ community, have been key to social movements promoting inclusion and cultural change. Like bonobos, cooperation and acceptance of diversity have been strategies for survival and the transformation of power. The connection between bonobos and homosexuality lies in the fact that both represent a form of social organization based on cooperation, diversity, and resistance to dominant power structures. From this perspective, one could argue that diversity—whether sexual, cultural, or migratory—is not a weakness, but rather a successful evolutionary strategy. A commercial diversification of the "Bonobo" name has also emerged, with clothing stores, bars, and nightclubs opening worldwide with special specifications for these human tastes and preferences.

Do you find any commonalities in the migration of these humans vs. non-humans?

Let's list more contributions to primate migration that can be identified with human migration:

- They prevent internal conflicts by renewing the composition of the group.
- They facilitate the exchange of behaviors and cultures between groups.
- They create broader networks between different communities.
- There is innovation and learning: new females bring new food gathering techniques, tool use, and parenting strategies.
- They share their knowledge about territories and resources with each other.
- Genetic variability increases.
- Reduces competition between relatives.
- Improves mating opportunities.
- Strengthens disease resistance in the population.
- They also have a significant ecological impact: they aid in seed dispersal between territories, maintain connectivity between

populations, and contribute to adaptability to environmental changes.
- Perhaps even more importantly, migrant females develop better social negotiation skills, greater adaptability, and many leadership abilities.

Do humans vs. non-humans need sex to gain or maintain power?

From an ethical standpoint, it's a no for humans! For chimpanzees and bonobos, it works differently. Let's explore some examples to find reasonableness, coherence, similarities, and differences between the symbiosis we're working on.

The tongue kiss, used by primates, is also used by humans. According to primatologist Frans de Waal, it is the bonobo's most recognized erotic act. The tongue is a highly sensitive organ that can contain sexual connotations. According to sexologist Tyomi Morgan, the surface of the tongue has a texture that makes it especially stimulating, as it generates a pleasurable friction, unlike what hands, lips, or other body parts could offer.

Bonobos are highly sexual. They use sex to get out of difficult situations, to get food, and to gain power. The alpha male enjoys all females. In humans, many people in power use it to sexually harass their subordinates. This connotation has changed: previously, it was only spoken of between men and women; today, it is a two-way street.

In *Immigrants Don't Eat Cats or Dogs* , one of our central themes is the exploration of human behavior from an evolutionary perspective, compared to non-humans. In this framework, power and hierarchy play a fundamental role, not only in survival and control of resources, but also in social and sexual dynamics. In many cases, in humans, although power shouldn't be translated into a tool of coercion, history and present-day reality show that it continues to be used to obtain sex in an abusive manner.

This abuse of power is directly linked to the vulnerability of immigrants and people in general. Just as subordinates in a corporate, military, or political hierarchy, in guerrilla groups, gangs, or religious sects can be forced to submit for fear of losing their status, position, or job security, they can also be subjected to a situation of sexual exploitation. The aggressor is always skilled at detecting victims who have few options for defense. It is a way of exercising power in a distorted way, just as it is used in politics to manipulate the weakest.

Politicians, campaigning for their bureaucratic positions, visit the neediest communities, where they have the greatest likelihood of winning votes. Their skill lies in identifying their greatest needs, analyzing their historical patterns, and their idiosyncrasies, in order to present development plans that, in most cases, go unfulfilled. They then give away groceries, bags of cement, and other materials; they bring road-fixing machines to impress them. They also make promises of scholarships and projects that are unattainable. As soon as they win their seats, their leadership operates behind closed doors.

Human society has developed value systems that should curb these abuses, but the instinct for dominance and power hinders these processes. The instinct for dominance is still present and, in some cases, is exercised without moral restraint. The difference between primates and humans lies not in the existence of abuse of power, but in the level of awareness and regulation that a society is willing to impose on these dynamics.

Looking ahead, the challenge—in both politics and migration—is to balance power with empathy and fairness, ensuring that hierarchical structures are not tools of abuse, but rather means for collective progress.

Divide and conquer

It has yielded excellent results for those who have applied it best. It is used to enable a specific government or structure to maintain power by fragmenting a potentially dangerous movement.

It can happen in two ways:

- First, those in power identify a strong group that could become dangerous to them. They then seek tactics to divide or fragment it. This weakens the group: it's easier to confront, manipulate, and control them.
- Second: whoever wants to seize power identifies the leader's strongest coalitions. As soon as they identify them, they begin the work of dividing them: "You move out so I can move in," the pecking order begins. This makes it easier to seize power.

Other forms of power expressed in humans can occur in powerful beings who don't necessarily have to be at the top of the structure, but who exert significant influence and control over the decisions made by those at the top. They can appear as peacemakers or strong in managing military strategy, or simply humanists and emotionalists, or others with a strong interest in promoting their own businesses.

We see the case of Elon Musk, the role he played early on in the current US government, and the current divergence with President Trump, now the founder of the new America Party political party, "divide and conquer," or Diosdado Cabello (the most wanted, Community of the Suns) in the current Venezuelan government, or what Eva Perón represented in Argentina in the context of a social leader and Peronism, a political and social movement that redefined the country. Another woman who greatly influenced Hitler's behavior and handling of power was his lover, Eva Braun.

In other areas, the "divide and conquer" approach in education can be used to fragment student movements and prevent unified protests. In the religious sphere, it has been used to generate sectarian conflicts and maintain control over the beliefs of the masses. Napoleon Bonaparte used this technique of conquest: he pitted European countries against each other so that he could attack them later, making it easier. Machiavelli also expressed it in his book *The Prince*: "Divide your enemies to weaken them and make them more manageable."

From another way of rising to power, we see how candidates, rulers, and presidents create imaginary enemies to divide the opposition, weaken their opponent, and win votes from both insecure voters and nationalist natives. In the case of the political phrase "immigrants are eating our dogs and cats," it was said that they were eating our pets. We all know that's not true. It was a political strategy to seize power: "divide and conquer."

We immigrants who have arrived in the United States and other host countries—not all of us, but the vast majority—are full of dreams. We are driven by hope and work. We contribute hard to the growth of these wonderful countries. We are productive. We immigrants don't eat dogs or cats.

Empathy between humans and non-humans

Oscar the cat, at the geriatric clinic in Providence, Rhode Island, is a fascinating example of the connection between humans and nonhumans in the context of caregiving and death. Oscar became famous for his ability to predict the deaths of patients. It is said that before someone passed away, he would lie down next to them and remain there until the end. His presence was so conscious that the medical staff began to recognize his behavior as a sign that a patient was in their final hours.

Empathy means "stretching out." It's the ability to put oneself in another's shoes, to understand and share another person's emotions, thoughts, or situations. It's also the ability to feel with another, to put oneself in their shoes, not only to understand their pain, but also their story; to stretch oneself to the limit, even to the unknown migrant, the animal, the child, the elderly, even the enemy. In the human context, empathy becomes a conscious act, a decision to connect, to include.

We could define empathy among non-humans as the ability of certain animals—especially those with complex social structures such as bonobos, chimpanzees, elephants, or dolphins—to recognize, share, and respond to the emotions of other individuals of their species, even of other species, without the need for verbal language, but through other actions, such as gestures, postures, compassion, solidarity, sharing, and suffering for others.

Empathy among non-humans is a lesson silenced by our arrogance. We've believed ourselves to be the only ones capable of loving, caring, and suffering for others. We've told ourselves the story that only we have souls, language, ethics... but nature has been practicing empathy without words for millions of years.

We don't notice—or have no records of—certain moments animals experience when they express it. For example: a group of dolphins accompanies one of their injured friends so it doesn't sink; there's no applause when two crows take turns feeding them; or when an elephant stops to stay by the body of a companion who's no longer breathing. Or the story of the dog Hachikō in Japan, who waited daily for his owner at Shibuya Station for almost 10 years after his death. Two blockbuster films were made about his noble story: one in Japanese in 1987, and another in English in 2009, starring Richard Gere. A statue is also part of his legacy of empathy. It stands at Shibuya Station in Tokyo. The second statue, from World War II, still stands today and is visited daily by tourists. It generates many emotions and has become an icon of loyalty.

Another story I want to share with you is that of our newest family member: a pug named Dogui. He came into our lives nine years ago. My wife, Gladys Monsalve, a transcendental woman in her love for her family, with maternal and protective feelings born from the womb of her soul, acquired him when he was just a baby. He seemed like a tiny ball of tenderness that only fit in our arms. We didn't know then that this little pug would become much more than a pet: he would be a silent witness to the growth of our family, a guardian of the most defenseless, the newest component to increase the happiness in our home. He was an inseparable companion to Andrey Fellype "Pipe," our youngest son—16 years old at the time—whose companion he was on his adventures and pranks. He also, simultaneously, accompanied our granddaughter Mariana Isabella, who was three years old at the time. Dogui never left her side. They played face-to-face, both of them like babies. When Dogui arrived, he had clumsy paws, a wet nose, and a look that seemed to understand everything. She looked at him curiously; he approached cautiously. They sniffed each other, and with their eyes, they chose each other without words. From that day on, they have been inseparable to this day. Then, three years later, a new member enters the scene: our grandson Gabriel Fellype, a very sweet and mischievous boy, who begins to identify his new best friend. And Dogui knew it. He approached slowly, as if instinct told him: "This one is mine too." Gabriel Fellype, who was just starting to walk, hugged him awkwardly and let out a short laugh, showing his first teeth. It was very sincere, enough to foster another strong bond between the two. Now, from a distance, after our migration to the United States, we make video calls to greet both Mariana Isabella and her lifelong friend Dogui. He leans closer to the camera every time we say his name. His anxiety is evident, as he can't locate us with his sense of smell—40 times more developed than ours. He tries, but the sea breezes, the high winds, and the distance prevent him from doing so. Despite having our pheromones, our voice, gestures, and energy formatted in his memory, we are certain he knows we exist. We always sense—as he surely senses—that we will soon be reunited. He is waiting for his family to return, having been forced to leave the country due to forced migration. He hopes they will return and we can reconnect in our natural habitat: our country, our city, our home. Because a dog's heart never forgets those it loves.

We clearly see how an emotional symbiosis is generated with our fellow planetmates. We could call it an *invisible symbiosis,* or what biology calls *a pact between species:* something that cannot be seen with a microscope, but in the heart. A bond that is clearly expressed when two beings need each other, not for their usefulness, but for an emotional and existential complement that strengthens the fibers of the spirit and brings happiness. A simple score that generates a feeling that could be called love.

We want to delve a little deeper into this dichotomy between humans and nonhumans to raise awareness of this relationship in the evolutionary process. To add a grain of sand to the appreciation of nonhumans. To see some characteristics that make us similar—and even identical—in some others. Nonhumans, in some ways, are on par with us in the evolutionary process. They have migrated with us, they have complemented the evolutionary process, and we are united by empathy.

Philosophy, empathy and evolution

We'll review some thinkers throughout history who have shown us a path of sensitivity and value toward non-humans, demonstrating their feelings, compassion, emotions, and empathy toward each other, as well as the shift in current positions in what they express toward humans.

- Theophrastus, the Greek philosopher (371 BC), said: "Animals can think, perceive, and feel like humans." "I refuse to eat them."
- René Descartes believed that animals were nothing more than automatons, without mind, soul, or reason. Later, laws were passed for their protection.
- Jeremy Bentham, the English philosopher (1748–1832), argued that neither reason nor discourse endows us with more rights than any other animal. The fact that we are capable of suffering and feeling pain is a sufficient criterion of equality to prevent them from being exploited. "If they suffer, their happiness and well-being are relevant."
- *Animal Liberation (1975),* Australian philosopher Peter Singer proposes a new ethic for our treatment of animals, applying morality and animal rights. Therefore, the interests of humans and animals must be given equal consideration.

Gary L. Francione: American author of numerous books and articles on animal ethics. He speaks about "the property status of animals" and argues that nonhuman animals require only one right: the right not to be considered property.

Frans de Waal: A prominent researcher in the field of primatology, a biologist and advocate of animal intelligence and emotions. He found parallels between human behavior and that of our earliest evolutionaries. He contributed to many studies of animal behavior and the relationship these aspects have with humans. Many behaviors previously attributed solely to humans—fairness, empathy, altruism, reciprocity, self-recognition, conflict resolution, mourning, and comforting—played a fundamental role in the acceptance of animal emotions as a valid line of scientific inquiry.

In 2010, the Cambridge Declaration on Consciousness was created. During the *Francis Memorial Conference,* held on July 7, 2012, thirteen neuroscientists from renowned institutions signed a manifesto affirming the existence of "consciousness" in various nonhuman animals. Converging evidence indicates that nonhuman animals possess the neuroanatomical, neurochemical, and neurophysiological substrates for conscious states, along with the capacity to exhibit intentional behaviors. Consequently, the bulk of evidence indicates that humans are not unique in possessing the neurological basis that gives rise to consciousness. Nonhuman animals—including all mammals, birds, and many other creatures, such as octopuses—also possess these neurological substrates.

Now, if human beings are viewed spiritually, from a spatial perspective, angels are above us, and animals are below us. This means that we are angels to them.

Having already reviewed the different schools of thought throughout history and what this sharing of experiences has meant for human beings, we see how empathy overlaps with many positions. As we might have a first perception: empathy is the best weapon to combat, for example, xenophobia. Human beings are xenophobic by nature. When we meet someone who doesn't identify with us, we mark a difference or distance ourselves; we are designed to hate those we don't like.

We will review several facets in this prospective. For example, non-humans have some advantages over us in terms of conflict resolution. Reconciliation in animals highlights empathy and demonstrates that it is not solely a human issue, but has deep roots in our shared evolution with other primates. After conflicts, primates reveal a surprising capacity for empathy and reconciliation. It is common to observe them hugging or grooming each other; elephants comfort a distressed member of the group. These displays are not accidental: they are part of restoring harmony within the group, reducing stress and strengthening social bonds.

There are many ways animals demonstrate empathy. For example, Frans de Waal found a community of chimpanzees in Mahale National Park, Tanzania, exhibiting a very special behavior: "social scratching." This behavior involves one monkey standing behind another and vigorously scratching its back a few times with its claws. This is key to understanding empathy as a social instinct.

It would be worth analyzing how the chimpanzee who is scratched feels relief, and how the scratcher knows how to interpret the precise spot where the itch is. It's a good question, isn't it? And for a good question, a good answer.

We continue…

We could associate it with a custom. We humans develop customs based on the environment we were raised in or the place where we live. For example, when we migrate, we have to adopt some of the customs of the place we arrive to. Why? To be accepted. We have to find a way to fit in. So we learn to speak like them, to simulate, to gesture. I remember a former boss's comment: "You have to learn to use our idioms; otherwise, it's very difficult for you to work with us."

Seventy percent of human communication stems from our gestures, that is, it's nonverbal. It stems from facial expressions. We can identify in our fellow humans: joy, sadness, surprise, fear, anger, disgust (the six basic emotions universally recognized by Paul Ekman). Now, this isn't just a human condition; nonhumans can also interpret them, both in their relationships with us and among themselves.

Let's name some examples:

- Chimpanzees bare their teeth in a grimace to express fear or submission, and their faces relax when they are calm, just like humans.
- Dogs lower their ears and crouch their bodies to indicate submission or fear; they wag their tails when they're happy. They've also learned to look humans in the eye to communicate needs or satisfaction, something they don't do with other dogs.
- Cats bristle their backs and enlarge their pupils to frighten or warn; when they need something or want to thank us, they brush their skin against ours.

Let's return to primate social scratching. If it were just a habit, then they'd adopt a stance that favors others more than themselves. But this particular action—Frans explains—requires knowing that others feel what you feel. Ultimately, there's no exact explanation, and it will remain unexplained. You certainly can't ask chimpanzees why they do it.

On the other hand, in another experiment, capuchin monkeys showed that these monkeys care about the well-being of their peers. In several situations, for example, a broom is left in a room. Someone points at it and they fetch it, but they ask for something in return, such as a treat. There is another bartering exercise with them that involves using plastic tokens.

The interesting thing, says the scientist, is when they were given a choice between tokens of different colors and meanings: one was selfish and the other prosocial. If the monkey chose the selfish token, it received a piece of apple as a reward, but its partner received nothing. If the monkey chose the prosocial token, both monkeys received the same reward.

What do you think happened?

The procedure was repeated many times, with different combinations of monkeys and sets of tokens. The result was always the same: they always chose the token that had food for both of them.

The moral of the story is: Monkeys like to eat in company, not alone. They like to do each other favors! If you both get food, you can sit at the table and share it together. It's just like us humans, right? We eat more happily when we sit at the table with family and friends.

Grooming: It's a social behavior between animals. One animal cleans the other's fur, removing dirt and insects, or simply gently touching it. But its function really goes beyond hygiene. It's a way of creating and strengthening social bonds between them. It's like saying, "I trust you, okay!", "We're okay!", "We're all in this!", "You're not alone!", "I care about you!"

It also helps promote cooperation and group stability, especially when there are conflicts or dangers. It's a form of early empathy. Grooming has also been shown to reduce stress. Nonhumans also suffer from stress like we humans. We'll revisit this point later when discussing the consequences of migration.

We wanted to take this condition into account because it applies to both. There's an effective regulator called empathy.

We humans don't call it grooming, but we do equivalent things, like:

- Embrace
- Combing a child's hair
- Caressing someone who is crying
- Holding the hand of an old man
- Look into the eyes with tenderness

Recognizing this changes the narrative: empathy doesn't make us human, but rather connects us to the nonhuman. This finding invites us to reflect on our own attitudes toward others. Humans haven't lost this capacity, but sometimes we bury it under layers of fear, prejudice, and misinformation, especially when confronted with the other... the different, the foreigner, the migrant.

If even animals seek reconciliation, why do we humans allow xenophobia to dominate us? Why do we cling to the rejection and prejudice of newcomers to our habitats?

CHAPTER 6

Violation of human and non-human rights

In the Auschwitz Holocaust: The Predecessor of Human Rights

This January 27, 2025, marks the 80th anniversary of the liberation of Auschwitz, the largest extermination camp in human history. Around 1.1 million people died there; the gas chambers and crematoria killed up to 5,000 people per day. The horror caused by the Nazi Holocaust and the massacre played a fundamental role in the adoption of the Universal Declaration of Human Rights in 1948.

This Universal Declaration, adopted by the United Nations General Assembly in 1948, was the first legal document to establish the universal protection of human rights.

According to the UN, human rights are rights inherent to all people, without distinction of race, sex, nationality, ethnic origin, language, religion, or any other condition.

Hitler's priority was to conquer Europe and create a pure race, without "contamination" from inferior races. Hitler is the greatest exterminator of the human race who ever existed. His army invaded many countries: among them Poland, Denmark, Norway, Belgium, the Netherlands, Luxembourg, Yugoslavia, and France. A human army is formed by a vertical chain of command; it is a well-synchronized structure, since close coordination entails absolute discipline. There is nothing more terrifying than a well-trained army, like Hitler's. He violated all inalienable human rights, minimizing them to the utmost. This surely makes him the greatest perpetrator of human rights abuses.

Dictators, conquerors, and manipulators always place armies on the right side of a society, maintaining coercion and force through arms. These hegemonies often violate the fundamental rights of their people. Militias are the dictators' first allies; one way or another, they win them over to their side. If they don't achieve this through pressure from the military courts—through insignia, decorations, and medals—they do so through favors for the highest-ranking commanders.

In the case of Venezuela, with the Cartel of the Suns, an alleged drug trafficking network involving high-ranking military officers, it has become the country with the most generals in its brigade and division ranks. Since President Nicolás Maduro came to power in 2013, a steady increase in military promotions has been observed. As of 2015, it was reported that 563 generals and admirals had been promoted: 189 in 2013, 229 in 2014, and 145 in 2015. Although exact figures may vary depending on the source, it is estimated that Venezuela currently has approximately 2,000 generals, even exceeding the combined number of generals in all NATO countries.

We would all think it's the most powerful army in the world... It isn't. It's the most bureaucratic. Let's remember the drone attack on Nicolás Maduro, as he addressed the people subjugated by his oppression, with his emotionally charged speeches, talking about the arrival of Venezuela's economic recovery. The soldiers in the parade broke ranks at the roar of the drones, as if they were anthropoids lacking the indoctrination of a command structure: without discipline, honor, or loyalty. They ran away from the scene, not exactly to defend their president.

From another perspective, and in line with the context of this study, we note that, apart from us, the only non-humans who possess an army are ants. They are the most ruthless armies. They have no generals or middle managers. Each soldier attacks or defends according to instinct, and has no qualms about dying in battle for their comrades, because they were born to fight and to fall in combat.

These insects have well-coordinated military strategies to protect their colonies, forage for food, or repel attacks from invaders. Ants can even be found forming alliances with mercenary species— similar, surely, to Erik Prince's army. They have demilitarized zones to avoid stepping into enemy territory. However , if an army of ants loses its way, following its own pheromone trail, they form a very tight ring in which thousands of them spin in circles until they die of exhaustion. Thanks to their vertical organization, this would never happen to humans.

Omar Albarracín

What does the Universal Declaration of Animal Rights, approved by the UN, say?

It establishes certain rights: the right to equality and existence, the right to respect, the right to attention, care and protection, the right to reproduce, the right to a reasonable limitation of the time and intensity of work, the right to not cause pain, the right to restorative food, the right to rest, and the right to a lifespan that is in accordance with their natural longevity.

No animal should be exploited for human enjoyment. Any act that involves the unnecessary death of an animal is biocide, that is, a crime against life. As a perspective, it's worth noting that these rights are aligned between humans and non-humans by the UN, the governing body of humanity.

From another perspective, the studies of scientists like Frans de Waal, who looked to the chimpanzee as a model, on primates that emphasized our violent side, may have similarities. But there is one aspect that humans manage that chimpanzees don't: in addition to war, we maintain peace.

For humans, managing peace is something as basic as drinking a glass of milk. Chimpanzees have nothing to give, as their inter-community relations are reduced to degrees of hostility. This means that to understand intergroup relations in humans at a more primitive level, we must go beyond the chimpanzee as an ancestral model.

Now, both humans and non-humans can ally themselves with the strongest group: yesterday we were best friends, today we are no longer. Today I switched sides, as politicians do in their famous coalitions. Now this new group defends its interests and attacks the other, to the death if necessary.

We put these arguments into context with our topic in this section of the study, which is human rights. These groups aren't just politicians or those in power—although one might think they would be our main focus. Well, they aren't just them, and they aren't all of them. There are other groups formed by the same social breakdown, which overwhelm the good people in a society. These are groups outside the law, such as common criminals, guerrillas, gangs, drug traffickers, criminal groups, human trafficking, child exploitation, paramilitaries, religious sects, and extremist political and governmental sectors against migrants. All of these groups, for the most part, violate human rights.

Wars and invasions cause massive human rights violations. Wars aren't usually caused by anger—it seems to run in our DNA. They often occur because leaders have political and economic interests; they want to expand their dominions and encompass more territory. Today, great powers seek to subjugate smaller countries, primarily through the pressure of economic blockades, the same technological capacity, high tariffs, and the blockade of the migrant community.

Violating human rights is not only about violating fundamental rights, guarantees, freedom, security, values, etc. It is also about trapping human beings in an ideological prison, whether political, religious, or other, in order to control them at the whim of whoever is in charge. These are often easily violated and manipulated in the collective unconscious.

The most absurd thing that can happen is when one becomes aware of oppression. Two situations arise: one, which is accepted out of one's own needs and fears; the other, due to the comfort level of the benefits it produces.

We have seen communities that have experienced the oppression and "satisfaction" of the communist government and the new socialism of the 21st century. The vast majority of them want to emigrate from their country. Many manage to do so; their own families help them with the human chains of migration. And after a few months, some want to return to their comfort zones. They struggle to understand that a capitalist system is about hard work, from sun to shade, where each person receives according to their own effort. Brilliant minds are probably the ones that stand out the most. That doesn't mean that those without them don't enjoy the same benefits, just on a lesser scale.

Scan the following QR code by Bayron Omar Albarracín Monsalve:

Part II Psychological consequences of migration

CHAPTER 7

In this second part of the book, we will explore the psychological consequences of migration, with special emphasis on the studies conducted by Dr. Joseba Achotegui, who presents migration under extreme conditions as Ulysses syndrome, a condition of extreme stress that affects those who face severe difficulties in the migration process. We will analyze the main stressors and factors that give rise to this syndrome and our own feedback on them. We will also address the seven griefs of migration, those inevitable losses that every migrant experiences and that require a process of adaptation to overcome. Without leaving aside the general context of this study, we will address the symbiosis that can also be generated in non-humans from an evolutionary perspective.

A migrant with Ulysses syndrome isn't crazy, but he or she suffers intensely. He or she cries inconsolably, can't sleep, has panic attacks, and suffers from physical pain with no apparent medical cause. Sometimes he or she isolates himself or herself. Sometimes he or she silently falls ill. Sometimes he or she works as if nothing is happening... until one day he or she collapses.

Ulysses syndrome

Ulysses to the Romans, Odysseus to the Greeks, was a king and hero who fought in the Trojan War and took a total of 20 years to return to his beloved homeland of Ithaca. Reference is made to the mythological hero who suffered loneliness and countless adversities: danger, hunger, sleep, forgetfulness, neglect... wandering outside his homeland and far from his loved ones, with the firm intention of returning to his true home. Penelope, which means "soul," represents that spiritual home.

After having overcome all obstacles—which are nothing more than overcoming our fears and inner conditioning—Ulysses inspires us to take that intrinsic journey of finding ourselves, which gives us a true sense of life and helps us achieve self-realization as human beings, diminishing fears and increasing values to overcome the "Trojan horse" within each of us.

That horse could be grief for family, stress that prevents improving one's quality of life, or the inability to find inner peace and happiness. In those days, people behaved like heroes in order to survive, but today the reality is different: people who emigrate from their country face risks perhaps greater than those taken by the Greek demigod Ulysses.

The reality is that we are mere mortals, flesh-and-blood human beings subjected to high risks in our lives, both individually and as families. It is, surely, that symbiosis between purpose and adversity.

Definition: Ulysses syndrome

Ulysses syndrome is a chronic, extreme stress disorder that affects many immigrants forced to leave their country and face extremely difficult living conditions at their destination. It was defined by Spanish psychiatrist Joseba Achotegui in 2002 and takes its name from the mythological character Ulysses, a symbol of the migrant who faces multiple adversities far from home.

In this chapter, talking about Ulysses syndrome means talking about those who endure in silence. Those who cry while washing dishes, caring for the elderly, driving trucks, harvesting fruit, cleaning houses, working in construction, in hotels, or in other tough jobs. It means giving a name to the pain that doesn't fit on a prescription or a work permit.

CHAPTER 8

Stressors and factors that lead to Ulysses syndrome

Stressors are external situations or conditions that generate a stress response in the body. These aren't simply everyday problems or worries, but rather factors that exceed an individual's ability to adapt, especially when they are multiple, intense, and prolonged.

It should be noted that Ulysses syndrome does not appear in any migrant, but in those who are subjected to the following factors:

1. Forced separation from loved ones, which involves a rupture of the attachment instinct

This stressor isn't simply a matter of geographical distance; it's an emotional rupture that undermines one of the most fundamental human bonds: attachment.

Psychiatrist John Bowlby, the father of attachment theory, demonstrated that emotional bonds are not just emotions, but biological. We are designed to bond with one another: with our parents, with our children, with our partners. It's a survival instinct. A child needs his mother to feel secure. An adult needs his family or partner to maintain his sense of belonging.

When this bond is abruptly broken—without goodbyes, without certainty of return—the brain could interpret it as a deep trauma.

For an immigrant, not being able to see their children grow up, leaving their sick parents behind, saying goodbye to their partner without knowing if they'll ever hug them again... All of this creates an invisible but constant wound. An unrelenting anxiety. A guilt that becomes a traveling companion.

There are always ways out... we must seek the strengths within ourselves. Physical separation from our loved ones can cause severe stress. Dr. Mario Alonso Puig, in his book *Volver a casa (Coming*

Home) , advises that, to be stronger, we must have a stronger spiritual connection with ourselves.

We must recover our essence and look within. One of the reasons may be that we have strayed far from the spiritual dimension. Human beings must connect with the essential: we have a body, but we are not just a body; we have a mind, but we are spirit.

We allow ourselves to be trapped in the material dimension. We are guided only by what our physical eyes show us. We ignore reality.

This inner journey gives us clarity, it gives us light. It doesn't give us darkness—as you're probably experiencing now—but what you truly are is that blue sky where the sun always shines.

You'll surely have to go through many dark nights away from your loved ones, from that bond of family... but you can't let yourself get frustrated. You must manage to see the light.

2. The feeling of hopelessness due to the failure of the migration project and the lack of opportunities

This second stressor, which crowns the pain of migration, is the feeling of failure. Migration is not a light adventure: it is a life project laden with expectations, dreams, sacrifices, and promises. When that project is not fulfilled—when the dream job is not found, when stability is not forthcoming, when family reunification is indefinitely postponed, when life becomes harder than in one's place of origin—a devastating shadow appears: hopelessness.

This stressor isn't just economic; it's deeply existential. The migrant feels like they've lost everything without gaining anything. They've left their family, uprooted their roots, faced discrimination, worked twice as hard for half the pay, and yet they still can't "get ahead." So the question arises: Was it worth it?

This grief paralyzes. The migration project becomes a prison without bars. There's no turning back, because returning unsuccessfully is also a form of symbolic death. But there's no moving forward either.

And in this emotional limbo, mental health deteriorates, strength is lost, and the feeling that there's no possible future sets in. That's the moment to seek help. You can't wait for the emotional situation to lead to making bad decisions.

3. The struggle for survival (where to find shelter, where to eat, where to live)

This third stressor is one of the most exhausting for immigrants: the daily struggle to survive. Something as basic as having a place to sleep, a hot meal, or a safe space becomes a constant challenge. Newcomers often find themselves without a support network, without savings, or stability.

This stressor generates a permanent state of alertness and physical and mental tension. People sleep little, eat poorly, and rest less. The body becomes exhausted and the mind dulls. Insecurity becomes a constant companion, and fear ceases to be a passing emotion and becomes a way of life.

4. The terror they experience in migratory displacements, the threats from mafias, the fear of being detained and expelled, the helplessness due to lack of rights, among others

This fourth stressor is also quite intense. Immigrants experience terror during the migration journey and upon arrival in the destination country. For many people, migration isn't a journey, it's a desperate escape: escaping war, hunger, domestic violence, or organized crime. But upon crossing borders, the danger doesn't end; it just changes its face.

The fear of being detained, deported, imprisoned, or separated from one's family—like what is currently happening in the United States, where many people, due to the violation of multilateral agreements with other countries, live with the daily anxiety of being deported—intensifies. But the deeper fear produced by this stressor is the risk of not being returned to our countries of origin, but to third countries that, for economic reasons, lend their prisons in exchange for charging high sums for each person locked in their cages.

Even worse is that innocent people see these rights violated—including the right to self-defense, which every human being has—simply because someone points the finger at them, without evidence, as part of organized criminal gangs.

5. The multiplicity of stressors: stressors reinforce each other

One of the most devastating factors of Ulysses syndrome is not a single stressor, but the combination and interaction of all of them. It's a series of simultaneous challenges that accumulate, intersect, and amplify each other.

The multitude of stressors generates an emotional and physical overload that exceeds the human capacity for adaptation. It's like trying to swim with a stone tied to your neck, then two, three... until you can't breathe anymore. The body becomes sick, the mind becomes exhausted, the soul withdraws.

Furthermore, these stressors are not static: they feed off each other. Fear fuels loneliness; discrimination undermines self-esteem; poverty reinforces hopelessness. And without access to mental health care, without a support network, without social or political legitimacy, without papers, the immigrant becomes a castaway on dry land.

6. Chronicity

Another stressor that can lead to Ulysses syndrome is the chronic nature of migration suffering. It's not just about going through difficult times during the migration process; what's truly impactful is that this pain never ends and continues over time, permanently impacting us.

At first, immigrants believe it's a temporary stage: better times will come, when I learn the language, when I get a job, when I legalize my status. But months pass, then years... and often conditions don't improve; they even worsen.

Chronic stress turns immigrants into people who no longer expect anything. They can fall into extreme psychological distress, requiring help. Dr. Achotegui created a foundation for these chronic stress levels, where people can find professional support: the Atenea Global Network. We'll look at its role with immigrants globally in more detail later.

This stressor also disrupts the possibility of healthy grieving. Because grief, by nature, requires closure, a step forward. But when the pain doesn't end, grief stagnates. It ends up becoming an endless spiral that prevents rebuilding.

7. The feeling that, no matter what he does, the individual cannot change his situation

This stressor is one of the most destructive in Ulysses syndrome: people develop the internal conviction that no matter what they do, nothing will change. This state is known as learned helplessness, a theory developed by Martin Seligman. It is a psychological phenomenon in which the individual, after multiple failed attempts to improve their situation, abandons all action, all struggle, all hope.

Learned helplessness is one of the greatest psychological dangers because it erodes self-esteem, destroys initiative, and prevents us from building a future. It leads to the perception that it's not worth continuing to try. This stressor is, therefore, a slow psychological death, which can lead to states of anxiety, deep depression, and even suicidal thoughts.

8. Deficits in their social support networks

This stressor, the lack of social networks, can cause high levels of stress in people. It is also true that migrant resilience has given rise to new forms of collective support, especially in communities that organize themselves to resist and rebuild. New support networks, both formal and informal, have been created, functioning as extended family, emotional community, and practical support.

In cities across the United States, Europe, and other host regions, it's common to find groups organized by nationality, region, or language: Colombians, Mexicans, Salvadorans, Haitians, Venezuelans, Nicaraguans, Chinese, Filipinos, Indians, Ukrainians... These groups meet in churches, markets, cultural centers, foundations, associations, WhatsApp groups, social media, NGOs, and even with the support of the governments themselves, generating a new network of support in exile.

9. Health systems

Inadequate treatment of this syndrome by the healthcare system, even racial discrimination, means that these immigrants are not correctly diagnosed as suffering from stress. Instead, they are treated as depressive, psychotic, or suffering from somatic disorders. In this case, the healthcare system becomes an additional stressor for immigrants.

We clearly see how many health professionals become another stage of pain, confusion, and invisibility. Furthermore, this psychological impact is not adequately recognized by these professionals. This situation reflects a profound lack of training in transcultural health and migration trauma.

Stressor feedback

"The paths of life are not as I thought, as I imagined them, they are not as I believed. The paths of life are very difficult to walk, difficult to walk them and I can't find the way out. I thought life was different; when I was little I believed things were easy like yesterday, that my good old lady tried hard to give me everything I needed, and today I realize that it is not so easy. Because my old lady is already tired of working for my brother and me, and now it's my turn to gladly help her, and for my old lady I will fight until the end!"

— (Colombian singer-songwriter Omar Geles)

Separation from our loved ones causes a rupture of the attachment instinct. The first strong bond formed in humans is probably from the gestation period, in that relationship with the mother through the umbilical cord, where she receives nourishment. This attachment figure creates a connection with the baby that gives it security and trust.

Aside from maternal attachment, other contexts emerge, such as their closest relatives: siblings, aunts, uncles, grandparents, cousins, and others. Also, those related to their childhood life role: their classmates, school, university, church, sports, food, smells, tastes, culture, and everything that makes up being human as part of a community and its homogeneous groups according to their preferences.

Now, the feeling of hopelessness due to the anxiety of the migration project failing and the lack of opportunities... The mere thought that migrants will be able to reach their destination and resolve their lives is overwhelming and generates emotional instability. Perceiving that they will not find alternative solutions to certain situations or that they have no concrete expectations for the future is often accompanied by an existential emptiness.

This state is often relieved by positive emotions such as feeling self-confident, experiencing serenity, joy, calm, peace, pleasure, as well as admiration and inspiration. That is, the emotional part that sustains us in the face of adversity.

The struggle for survival, for finding food and shelter, is arguably one of the most ambivalent stressors for migrants. It is one of humankind's greatest concerns. Although the brain is programmed to face the greatest obstacles in the most unpredictable circumstances, if we manage to adapt to this stressor, we act with greater confidence and security.

The terror of displacement: people who cross borders illegally always face long journeys. The unpredictability of nighttime travel, crossing deserts, rivers, and oceans, traveling in trucks or buses, sleeping in overcrowded conditions... They face multiple risks, both from the mafias that operate the border trade—coyotes, criminal groups, and criminal gangs—and from border patrol officers and immigration officials, who often take advantage of migrants' uncertainty to extort them and, in some cases, abuse children and women.

Typically, these situations do not come to light and become part of a pact of silence.

The multiple stressors refer to the different stimuli capable of provoking a stress response. Stress is that very response or reaction to a stressor. These definitions show that stress is individual, as stimuli can generate different reactions in two people, even if they face the same situation.

The more stressful situations exist, the more they reinforce each other and the greater the impact on each migrant's individual situation.

Chronic stress, which many people experience when they don't overcome their long-term conditions, typically progresses slowly over time. In other words, any type of stress that persists for weeks or months becomes chronic stress.

This situation can have a devastating impact on an immigrant's mental and physical health. Some signs that stress may be affecting them include diarrhea, constipation, poor memory, body aches, headaches, lack of energy and concentration, sexual problems, hair loss, a stiff neck or jaw, and fatigue. All of this increases the risk of heart disease, diabetes, obesity, and other chronic illnesses.

There are people who find it difficult to overcome their current situation.

They could be called stubborn or headstrong because they have decided they will do what they want and refuse to do anything else. It is possible to say that the emotional reaction does not match the actual or current circumstances. According to the author Viktor Frankl, an Austrian neurologist, psychiatrist, and philosopher, who survived four Nazi concentration camps, he put forward a thesis on this idea, saying: "When we are no longer able to change a situation, we are faced with the challenge of changing ourselves."

Frankl meant that, despite the most adverse circumstances, it is possible to live a positive and meaningful life, and he encouraged us to seek out novelty and to conceive it with creativity and responsibility, especially in times of crisis.

The deficits in their support networks

Some personal characteristics of those considering mobility could be considered. Among the most important is defining human capital at the individual level, with variables such as professional qualifications, family educational level, work experience, and so on. These variables position migrants differently when comparing their capabilities. From a psychological perspective, this refers to the greater or lesser capacity migrants have to confront problems without seeking support from others.

Support networks will function in different ways. We understand that human beings have the capacity to learn independently; however, by nature, they are social and political beings. Hence, the need to connect with others, to gain knowledge of other social systems, with the same or different languages, with different behaviors: their social institutions, politics, culture, religion, new work practices (such as hourly pay, weekly pay, etc.).

From this perspective, a knowledge accumulation begins, allowing the migrant to make definitive decisions that profoundly affect their current situation. From these clues, the idea of embarking on the journey is formed. At this stage, the support network is reduced to the family group: parents, siblings, aunts, uncles, cousins, and friends, who become the first to support the process.

When you are already an immigrant

That is, once you're on the other side, identity traits are formed. People with characteristics specific to a community come from the same place, municipality, city, country, university, sports team, church, or company. In this type of support network, solidarity predominates. For example, when someone dies or falls ill, there is support both in the place of origin and in the destination.

Other identity links include beliefs, sports interests, etc. Likewise, social networks are built through employment to defend migrant rights.

Psychological support

Many health professionals misjudge immigrants, trivializing the full picture. They often issue diagnoses that are far from reality, categorizing them as having somatic illnesses. This happens due to ignorance, insensitivity, racism, or xenophobia.

If a disorder truly exists, it would be best to seek appropriate follow-up and treatment to improve the extreme anxiety caused by physical symptoms. These thoughts and feelings block people, causing them to feel unable to perform their daily activities.

Misdiagnoses

When patients are diagnosed with depression, with symptoms such as memory problems, personality changes, physical pain, fatigue, loss of appetite, sleep problems, headaches, or thoughts of death or suicide, this indicates that the psychological condition is advanced and requires treatment.

Another diagnosis is psychosis, which occurs when people suffer from a set of symptoms that affect the mind and cause them to lose some contact with reality.

Medical support for immigrants is increasingly limited, with increasing demands placed on them by the physical and mental health systems of host countries. In some cases, it is downright exclusionary.

We need to work hard in this direction. Great credit is due to Dr. Joseba Achotegui and the Atenea Foundation for their work saving lives worldwide.

Functional medicine and migrant stress

Dr. Carlos Jaramillo is a Colombian physician specializing in functional medicine and nutritional biochemistry. He has provided guidance on these topics through his YouTube channel and worldwide lectures. He has written several books, including *Anti-Stress* and *The Art of Eating Well to Be Well* .

He recounts how he was on the verge of death from stress, which caused meningitis due to an immune system destroyed by depression, guilt, and frustration. This confirms the close connection between psychological and physical health.

The vision of Dr. Carlos Jaramillo

According to Dr. Jaramillo, stress is normal and necessary. Every stage of life brings its own stressors, as is the case with immigrants. The body is a system that is ready and prepared to respond to them. Therefore, stress can help us be productive, energize us, and empower us on the journey. The downside is letting it go beyond its limits and allowing it to become chronic.

He explains stress with two special phenomena of our body:

1. Homeostasis

It is the process by which the body maintains a stable internal balance, despite changes in the external environment. It is essential for the body to function properly: maintaining body temperature around 37°C, blood sugar levels, water and salt control, maintaining blood pH within a specific range, etc.

2. Allostasis

It is the process by which the body actively adapts to internal and external changes to maintain balance and survive. This occurs when we reach such a high level that we are unable to return to a normal state.

When the body is forced to constantly adapt to stressors (emotional, physical, social), it pays a price: allostatic load.

When this load is very high and sustained over time, people begin to get sick. Excessive allostatic load can lead to:

- Insomnia
- Anxiety or depression
- Inflammatory diseases
- Chronic fatigue
- Loss of memory or concentration

And in severe cases: Ulysses Syndrome.

It's not stress that kills us, it's our reaction to it.

— Hans Selye

Everything indicates that the scientific level is aligned with these theories. From another perspective, the Austro-Hungarian Dr. Hans Selye, in studies conducted in the 1930s and 1940s—considered the father of stress studies—defined stress as the body's adaptive response to different stressors. He called it General Adaptation Syndrome (GAS). The word "stress" comes from the Greek *stringere* , meaning "to cause tension."

What do we mean by stressors? They are circumstances, unforeseen situations, or setbacks—personal conditions, cohabitation, migration, work or professional—that occur in our lives and that we perceive, consciously or unconsciously, as a threat or difficulty; in short, what we experience as something negative. It's about the body adapting to the dynamics of everyday life. Our nervous system doesn't distinguish between a real, physical stressor and a merely mental one.

Hans Selye discovered two types of stress. One is necessary in life: to grow, improve, as a stimulant to advance, learn new things, take on challenges like migration and how to cope with them. The other type of stress, to which he dedicated much of his life, is distress, which refers to a negative or exaggerated response to stressors, whether biological, physical, or psychological.

Distress is chronic stress, very similar to the theory of Ulysses Syndrome proposed by Joseba Achotegui. It is a sustained form of stress that leaves no room for a human being to recover or renew itself. It is profoundly damaging to health in all three dimensions: body, mind, and emotional dimension.

CHAPTER 9

Do animals suffer from stress?

The answer is yes. And who causes these stressors in non-humans? In most cases, it's us humans. Through ecosystem destruction, deforestation, climate change, abandonment, illegal trafficking of species, abuse, or simply selfishness disguised as indifference.

Also when we drag them along with us in our migratory processes without understanding that they, too, are leaving behind a familiar world. That they, too, have memories, attachments, routines, and emotions. Changes that are challenging for us can be overwhelming and incomprehensible for them. They experience the journey as a rupture, experiencing their own grief for the lost territory, for the familiar smell that is no longer there, for the silence of the companion left behind. Stress doesn't distinguish between species; it only reacts to loss, fear, and uncertainty.

Non-human migrants also have their own stressors, just like humans. This post-traumatic stress doesn't distinguish between species. Changes can affect us all equally: a dog that changes homes, a bird that no longer finds the tree where it nested, or a person who has left their country. The body and mind respond with anxiety, behavioral changes, physical illness, or depression, which can lead to Ulysses Syndrome.

In the animal kingdom, stress doesn't only come from the environment or human actions. Stress also arises among animals, such as from competition, hierarchies, struggles for territory, food, or simply ignorance of others, which can lead to conflict.

And in the context of displacement or migration, it's also causal. Trauma is contagious: a stressed animal can stress the group, just as an individual who has experienced violence can become reactive, and their behavior disrupts the peace of others.

But there's also another side... a way out, at least a response, a rationale: just as stress can be contagious, so can calm. Just as a group can reject, it can also welcome. Many animals, after a few days, accept new members, share food, groom each other, and learn to live together.

Likewise, human communities can learn to integrate, to reach out, to understand that the newcomer doesn't come to take away, but rather to seek the same thing as everyone else: a dignified life.

CHAPTER 10

The 7 duels of migration according to Joseba Achotegui

Grief can be compared to squeezing the walls of the heart at its four corners.

Migration is much more than moving. It is perhaps losing in order to reinvent oneself. Migrants, as Dr. Joseba Achotegui puts it, face up to seven simultaneous griefs that shake their emotional structure.

In the context of this book, we want to convey that these griefs are not exclusive to humans. Nonhumans—domesticated and wild animals—also experience their own griefs when ecosystems change, when homes crumble, when bonds are severed. Migration, in essence, is a shared experience.

1. Grief for family and loved ones

Family and loved ones are perhaps the most vulnerable in separations. Perhaps the emptiness we experience within us will never be repaired. It's a grief we endure daily: the loneliness, the inner crying of our hearts, the hug and blessing from mom and dad upon leaving and upon arriving home, the sharing with siblings.

Who will replace that sibling in their daily chores? You'll no longer be able to say, *"I did it yesterday."* Sitting around the table together, savoring that warm meal, laughing, sharing stories from the day, asking your child, looking them in the eye, *"How was school?"* Making sure they ate their snack, that their shoes and clothes were clean...

As for the elderly parents you left behind in your country, just wondering if they've taken their medications, who will accompany them to their medical appointments... These parents surely look forward to the dawn of day, hoping to see you soon. When someone knocks on their door, they quickly get up and leave their chairs; perhaps they were watching television or simply coping with the pain in their bodies. They open the door, their faces increasingly marked by the lines of time, drawing your image in their thoughts, believing you're coming back.

Remembering from when you were a child to what you may be today, those parents would give everything they have to have you for a moment, to be able to hold you and say, *"You're part of my insides. You're a part of me."*

The reality is that it was all a mirage that passes through their thoughts perhaps daily. They end up standing on the porch, looking in two directions, left and right, unfathomably. With sadness reflected in their souls, they see you coming, frowning, their eyes watering as they realize you haven't returned yet... and perhaps you never will. Only a deep sigh rubs their ribcage to replenish the air in their lungs, regaining a new strength that frames their existence as they feel that mournful emptiness in their hearts.

Professor Achotegui explains that these forced separations result in great psychological suffering, which increases the risk of developing a mental disorder, especially in children. These children find it difficult to forgive the intense suffering they have experienced and are often cruel in their treatment of their parents. They seek revenge for the abandonment they suffered when they return to live together after family reunification.

These families, separated for a long time, are like a broken vase. It's not easy to put all the pieces back together. It requires a lot of support, good conditions, and stability. If these conditions aren't met, the family ends up breaking apart.

In today's world, thanks to globalization and technological advancements, social media has made it possible to improve these relationships between parents and children. Interconnectivity allows for virtual closeness between people through social media, text messages, voice calls, and video calls.

But let's remember that children aren't postal packages. They suffer abuse, sexual abuse, and labor exploitation, given their defenseless state.

Unfortunately, there aren't many institutions dedicated to restoring this emotional element, although host countries design psychological support through schools, churches, migrant social networks, and organizations in host countries that contribute to these processes.

2. The duel for the language

Language grief is one of the most silent, yet profound, aspects of the migration process. Joseba Achotegui defines it as the loss of one's native language in the migrant's everyday life. It's not about learning new words, but rather feeling that one's own words are no longer useful. Their emotions, their memories, their ideas are encapsulated in a language no one around them understands. It's as if their soul has fallen silent.

Your mother tongue isn't just a tool of communication; it's an emotional territory. It's how you learned to name love, fear, and nostalgia. It's what you used to talk at home, to sing in the shower, to pray, or even to insult when something went wrong. It's the language of dreams. Migrating means facing an environment where that language no longer resonates. Where everything sounds foreign, even your own voice.

This grief has many faces. The most obvious: lack of communication. We fear misspeaking, being judged by our accent, using inappropriate words. Migrants often censor ourselves, remaining silent so as not to be mocked or singled out. In many cases, we isolate ourselves, because linguistic loneliness is as harsh as geographical loneliness: we can't find the right location.

We experience many situations, for example, remaining silent at a party, at school, in a meeting, or even at work, because we don't understand the conversations. Then we feel out of place. The powerlessness is so great, as if life were passing us by without inviting us to participate.

As we've always said, there are always ways out. It all depends on each individual: their desire to improve and their ability to adapt. In the United States, for example, there are public schools that offer classes at different times so people can learn the language. Typically, they offer three hours a day, free of charge, without paying a single dollar. It's about allocating your time and taking advantage of the available tools.

And there are many more options: online courses, training in their field of study, and everything the internet offers. From a psychological perspective, this process has positive effects. When migrants feel capable of communicating, of expressing what they feel, what they need, their self-esteem is immediately strengthened. A sense of belonging is restored. Words once again become bridges, not barriers. They become translators of experiences, a link between realities.

This developed skill gives you a new identity: richer, more open, with more possibilities, more job opportunities, more interpersonal relationships, more versatility, and much more openness toward others.

3. Mourning for culture

According to Professor Achotegui, culture can be viewed from a broader perspective, encompassing values, worldview, eating habits, leisure or free time, dress, religion, customs, and more.

Language is closely associated with culture, but they are not the same. Just as a Colombian and a Mexican speak the same language, but are from different cultures. The changes that immigrants experience when confronting a new culture generate stress related to these aspects, which is called acculturative stress.

However, other factors are more relevant today, such as family and social stressors. There is a close relationship between these, as social conflicts are often expressed through culture and identity. Immigrants experience certain complexities regarding their culture of origin and the culture of the host country.

It's how many of us begin to appreciate culture, its folklore, its habits, and customs only after we've left. A specific case in point is that of a Bolivian immigrant who joined a traditional dance group, which—as she herself admits—she didn't appreciate when she lived in her country. But today she says, *"Through folklore, I bring a little piece of my homeland, of Bolivia."*

From a psychological perspective, it can be said that assimilation and integration require immigrants to admire the host culture, learn to identify with it, and appreciate it. It has been pointed out that many Latinos find it difficult to adapt to the Anglo-Saxon way of life, as they perceive it to have fewer family values and to focus more on material things, based on the premise that Latinos are more extroverted and cheerful people.

According to Achotegui, all cultures have something in common. From this perspective of interculturality, there are more universal aspects that unite us than those that separate us. He explains that there are no completely different cultures A and B, but rather that each of them is the result of interactions throughout history.

In today's world, we all participate in a global culture. We are all part of a large substructure, or a single mode of production in the Marxist sense (or non-production, due to the number of people who become unemployed, many of them immigrants), with a culture that is the superstructure, defined as all the organs and institutions of a society, which, through certain ideologies and policies, shape the ideas followed by a community. Marx defines it as the basis of society.

Different cultures have their own ways of expressing grief, even in colors. In China, India, and Japan, the color white is used for mourning; in classical Rome, red; in Syria, blue; in Mexico, sky blue; in the United States, black; in Egypt, orange and yellow; in Great Britain, blue; and in Thailand, violet, among others.

Regarding values, they are highly inclusive: tradition emphasizes the importance of ancestors. Religiousness is highly influential in the elaboration of migratory grief, given that it provides individuals with an explanation for their difficulties and suffering, offering the possibility of shared rituals for grieving , fostering the development of social capital, which is of great importance for migrant integration.

From a religious perspective, grief can be complicated or extreme when immigrants struggle to express their culture. This is the case for many Muslim immigrants who practice the Abrahamic, monotheistic religion of Islam, who struggle to carry out their religious practices, such as building mosques or making the pilgrimage to Mecca.

Western culture is characterized by an extreme focus on time, as part of social success. This appreciation of time is also a relational part of culture. So much so that in the United States, there is a city called Rapid City, located in Pennington County, South Dakota. In other words, it is identified with the way of doing things: quickly.

Another frequently mentioned case is that, in Africa, you can tell from the way people walk whether they've been to Europe. Or, when we see an American and a British person, just by listening to them speak, we know their nationality.

As globalization has grown, acculturative stress has also changed. Achotegui explains that perhaps it's more complex today because, while we experience the cultural shift from one country to another, the truth is that we're all already part of the same global consumer society.

4. Mourning for the land

According to Dr. Joseba Achotegui's contributions in the book *Migratory Intelligence*, the Earth encompasses the landscape, the colors, the smells, the light. All of these aspects affect individuals during migration, especially when they move to dark and cold places. Considering human evolution—we all come from Africa—it's been a little over 100,000 years since we left there, where the climates were warm. From that perspective, studies on happiness show that people who live in these climates are happier.

Migrants must deal with two situations in this regard. One is to process grief with aspects linked to the land they leave behind; this grief indicates that we have not yet fully adapted to cold and dark climates, far from our warm African cradle. Body temperature also plays an important role in climate adaptation. Since we come from Africa, the temperature to which our cold/heat receptors are believed to be adapted is 27.7 degrees Celsius, the average temperature of the African plain for millions of years.

Brightness also influences mood, as the optic nerve is connected to the limbic areas of the brain. It is also linked to the early onset of menarche—the arrival of the first menstrual period—an important milestone in any girl's life. It normally occurs between the ages of 10 and 15, when all parts of the reproductive system have matured. In sub-Saharan Africa, it can occur as early as age 9, while in the Inuit (indigenous people who live in the tundras of northern Canada, Alaska, and Greenland), it can be delayed until age 19, due to the influence of light on sex hormones.

Achotegui also explains the topic of smells, which are linked to relevant biological aspects related to the rhinencephalon or primitive brain (the part of the brain that processes smells and emotions). Smell is the key to memory. Smells trigger strong memories, as they are processed in the same brain areas responsible for emotions, learning, and memory. Some of Dr. Achotegui's immigrant patients have explained that, to experience odor sensations similar to those in their homeland, they would wander around the entire city to which they had emigrated.

The second situation is the stress of facing the host country. According to Achotegui, the land plays a more important role for people than a simple physical map. It's not something abstract, but a source: like a tree, that childhood square, that "homeland" that remains deeply imprinted in our subconscious.

5. Grief over social status: papers, work, housing, opportunities for social advancement

Professor Achotegui refers to social status as everything related to work papers, housing, and access to opportunities. He explains that, in general, migration seeks to improve not only economic status, but also access to cultural assets and freedom. According to him, immigrants lose their status through migration. That is, upon arriving in a new place, the status they had in their home country is not always upheld, and they must take on tasks that are not commensurate with their training. If years pass and they fail to reaffirm this status, they become demoralized and enter a crisis, which can deepen migratory grief, especially among undocumented immigrants. This extreme grief related to status is one of the foundations of Ulysses syndrome.

Studies show that many immigrants who worked in more than 40 professions in their country of origin can only access four or five jobs in their host country, and at very low professional levels.

"It's 4:30 a.m. The clock chimes. Marta wakes up in her humble boarding house, looking lovingly at her bed, because her little boy is sleeping in the corner. She hasn't slept well for several nights. She's short on money, and it's hard to work. Two months' rent is almost three. She's a single mother and can't pay, but she gets ready quickly and has a coffee. She feels like her little boy is about to wake up. Her wet eyes try to hide; she hates that Pedrito sees her cry... Marta crosses the city in her eagerness to work. Positive, she thinks that today she's going to clean a house... The day passes, and there's nothing to do. Between tears and loneliness, she returns home just like yesterday... she didn't bring a single rial."

(Lyrics from "Marta", a song composed by Heredero, Colombia)

In the book *"The Illusion of the American Dream,"* written by Mexican immigrant Lupita Hernández—an immigrant to the United States who worked as a cleaner and in hotels to survive without legal social status—she recounts the hardships and forced labor she faced. She recounts how she was pressured to complete her tasks, with excessive workloads, simply for not having legal papers. Lupita recounts how *managers* yelled at her simply for being Mexican. The responses she received when she complained were always that "they didn't meet job expectations," but, according to her, the truth was that Mexicans didn't complain because they were in a state of legal vulnerability, which allowed for abuses.

What were those abuses?

Lupita says they were assigned tasks that residents didn't want to do, and were constantly pressured to complete them quickly, despite being overworked. She points out that managers were unprepared to handle people, who had only learned their duties through practice. In fast-food restaurants, for example, there is high staff turnover precisely because of mistreatment. It's similar to the treatment received by farmworkers, cooks, housecleaners, and hotel staff, whose jobs are grueling and poorly paid.

Lupita invites President Donald Trump to visit restaurant kitchens, hotels, construction sites, farms, and factories to verify that those working there are Mexican and Latin American immigrants. It's another story that confirms that immigrants don't eat dogs or cats. We come to work, to contribute to the system, to contribute our part in the symbiosis.

In her hotel work, Lupita says they are required to clean rooms quickly, especially in the summer. They are pressured by *managers* to do it in less than 20 minutes, and are often assigned up to 21 rooms per day, a superhuman workload.

Like what Lupita, or Marta in the song "Heir" experienced, is the daily life of many immigrants. That's where the grieving process begins: when one ceases to be who one was, not because one wants to reinvent oneself, but because the system reduces one to what it allows. Identity fractures. Self-esteem weakens. A sense of worthlessness, regression, and injustice develops. The immigrant sees themselves as someone who had to abandon their potential at customs, or after crossing the Rio Grande, at the airport, or at the bottom of a box with diplomas that are no longer useful.

Always ways out...

Despite this grief, many migrants continue to move forward. We don't stop. We don't give up. We work twice as hard, we learn, we reinvent ourselves. We become bigger, stronger—as Shakira says. It doesn't matter that the world doesn't see us that way. We are. Because that status may have changed, but our value hasn't.

Over time, we can recover what was lost, build something new, deeper, and even better than the native ones. We overcome these "human crocodiles"; they don't affect us. Our mental spectrum opens up. We can see new horizons, with greater eagerness, a greater desire to improve ourselves, even creating great ventures where we even employ those who previously despised us.

According to the American Immigration Council, statistics show who immigrants are in the United States: more than 20% of new businesses are founded by immigrants, who represent approximately 14–15% of the total population. In sectors such as accommodation and food services, immigrants make up about a third of entrepreneurs, and in construction, approximately 26.6%.

Furthermore, 46% of the companies on the Fortune 500 list (ranking established by *Fortune magazine* in 2024) were founded by immigrants or children of immigrants.

Other countries:

- United Kingdom: Immigrants represent approximately 14% of the population and have established around 14% of new businesses in the last decade.
- Germany: With an immigrant population of 15%, it is estimated that immigrants have founded around 20% of new businesses in the last 10 years.
- France: Immigrants make up approximately 13% of the population and have created nearly 12% of new businesses in the last decade.
- Hong Kong: Immigrants represent nearly 38% of the population and have founded around 25% of new businesses in the last 10 years, particularly in trade and services.

6. Grief due to contact with the group of belonging: prejudice, xenophobia, racism

People often experience collateral damage when they identify with certain groups in their place of origin; during migration, this identification changes when they interact with other groups. Immigrants must grieve for the reduction or loss of contact with their group of origin, and at the same time, when they come into contact with a new group of origin.

From an anthropological perspective, Professor Achotegui explains that human beings, in their evolutionary process, demonstrate that all human groups have certain prejudices toward other groups. In this evolution, we have seen how humans have lived much of our history in small groups, family clans in constant competition with other similar groups for very scarce survival resources. At that time, survival outside the group was impossible, which left us with a strong need to belong to a group and a tendency to develop prejudices toward others.

The problem arises when these behaviors escalate into xenophobia or racism. High levels of prejudice lead to both of these scenarios, which make it difficult to grieve for the group to which the immigrant belonged. In any case, for many immigrants, the terms "integration," "assimilation," and "multiculturalism" are just nice words that hide the same social exclusion.

Professor Achotegui explains, quoting Jafo Karen: "Racism is in the common sense of white people." There have been centuries of colonialism, of justifying that there were people who could be treated as inferior because they weren't like white people. He writes in his book *Migratory Intelligence* that we cannot forget that not even twenty years ago there was a stuffed black man in a museum in Spain, in Banyoles. It's an example of the deep-rooted level of discrimination against Africans.

7. Grief for physical risks

This grief is one of the hardest and least visible: the grief caused by physical risks. This grief not only affects the migrant's soul or psyche, but also directly affects their body, their life, their integrity.

While other griefs involve emotions, language, identity, status, or family, this last grief pierces the skin. It is the rawest, the most physical. The grief that hurts with hunger, bleeds at the border, in shelters, drowns in the sea or rivers, freezes in deserts. The grief that can not only break the migrant, but also kill him.

Professor Joseba Achotegui points out that this grief goes beyond the psychological because it involves the migrant's very life. There are no metaphors here. There are realities: trains where bodies fall, jungles like the Darién where women disappear, children and the elderly die. There are detention camps, refugee camps, prisons like the CECOT in El Salvador, where each deportee is worth a monetary sum. There are concrete walls like those in Mexico and the United States, electric fences, medical exclusion, labor and sexual exploitation, xenophobic violence. This is the price of invisibility.

Migration has become, in many parts of the world, a question of placing one's body as an offering on an uncertain altar, hoping the journey doesn't cost more than one is willing to give, turning into a pilgrimage where some don't arrive, but all are transformed.

Non-humans also migrate for many reasons, as we have reviewed throughout this discussion—and any others that may be worth considering—suddenly locked in cages, working animals, or used as commodities, in the jungle, the sea, and the cities. They too are in physical danger, they too suffer, they too die. While they don't understand the political, economic, or psychological reasons for exile, they feel the pain in their flesh just as we do. The big difference is that they can't tell the story, like writing books about migratory grief.

Feedback from the seven griefs of migration

The seven griefs of migration that Professor Joseba Achotegui presents are open wounds in the migrant's emotional body. And yet, each of them can also become a scar with dignity, a story worth telling, proof that, despite the loss, we remain standing.

On this journey, we often believe we are walking alone. But that's not the case. Beside us, closer than we think... other beings also migrate: non-humans. They too leave behind their habitats, their group, their role within the pack, their codes, their voice, their freedom. They too suffer. They too miss.

Perhaps therein lies the key to the journey, as if it were one: understanding that the pain of migration is not exclusive to human beings. That there is a symbiosis, that close and lasting relationship between humans and non-humans, who—despite being of different species—live together in close proximity. It endures over time in our evolutionary process, experiencing an emotional parallelism that brings us ever closer.

Because if there's one thing that unites us, it's our resilience, our ability to adapt without forgetting who we are, our ability to trust again, to nest on a new branch, to howl on another mountain, to dance in another land... always remembering our own.

CHAPTER 11

Goddess Athena

In Greek mythology, Athena is the protector of Odysseus. She helps him return home. She was the goddess of wisdom, war, crafts, strategy, and justice; the favorite daughter of Zeus, the bravest and most resourceful of the Olympian gods. She is portrayed as a companion of heroes, the protective goddess of heroic endeavor. She is Odysseus's main ally during his long and painful journey home after the Trojan War. She doesn't spare him from suffering, but she doesn't abandon him either: she cunningly accompanies him, guides him in moments of doubt, and supports him when pain threatens to rob him of his identity.

Atenea Network Foundation

This foundation evokes Athena, the Greek goddess of wisdom, but also of justice, strategy, and the protection of the most vulnerable. And that is what it represents in the contemporary migration context: a beacon of clarity amidst emotional devastation. Credit must be given to the Red Atenea Foundation and the people who work there, with a high degree of human sensitivity, as well as to Professor Joseba Achotegui, its founder, for supporting the dignity of immigrants internationally.

The network was founded at the World Psychiatric Association's Congress *on Migration, Mental Health, and Transculturality in the 21st Century,* held from October 30 to November 1, 2010. It emerged as an initiative of the Ulysses Syndrome Program at the University of Barcelona and the School of Public Health at the University of California, Berkeley; institutions with a long history of working on the mental health of immigrants.

The Atenea Network is a global network of psychological support for migrants in extreme situations. It is a space for sharing experiences, research, and initiatives aimed at improving the mental health of migrants.

"Psychological help should not seek to normalize the person, but rather to free them from everything that makes it difficult for them to find their own path, as well as from the shackles of mental illness."

In the context of the main topic of our study, *"Immigrants don't eat cats or dogs ,"* the Atenea Network serves as a great support for all those who may need it at some point. It is a non-profit organization dedicated to promoting the social inclusion of people in situations of or at risk of exclusion. Its areas of intervention include employment, drugs and addictions, social inclusion, children and families, civic participation, deprivation of liberty, and housing. The foundation also carries out initiatives in research, consulting, training, and awareness-raising.

The Atenea Network was born out of two urgent needs: on the one hand, the increasing number of extreme and dangerous situations to which migrants are subjected; on the other, the existing gaps in support networks. The Atenea Network recognizes that immigrants are stewards of cultural diversity. It also holds worldwide conferences to receive contributions and feedback, with the goal of continuing to support immigrants globally.

To contact the Athena Network:

- Website: www.laredatenea.com
- Email: laredatenea2010@gmail.com

It currently operates in the following countries: Spain, the United Kingdom, Germany, Belgium, France, Italy, Japan, Mexico, and the United States.

Part III. Migratory Ecstasy

CHAPTER 12

The ecstasy of migration is the satisfaction of overcoming the challenges presented, to the extent that a profound transformation is achieved within each of us, after having experienced pain, uprooting, adaptation, and the struggle for dignity. It is savoring the immense emotion produced by the result, the success, and the achievement of our purpose, redefining our own experience as part of a personal and collective evolutionary process.

Jesus the Stranger

Pope Francis, Jorge Mario Bergoglio, the son of Italian immigrants in Argentina—who died precisely as we share this spiritual reconversion, on April 21, 2025—dedicated a significant part of his pontificate to the defense of migrants and refugees. In various messages and speeches, he advocated for a more inclusive Catholic Church and humanity, recognizing Christ himself in migrants.

Referring to Jesus:

"He himself told us. He is the one knocking at the door: hungry, thirsty, a stranger, naked, sick, and imprisoned, asking us to find him and help him. Migrants are missionaries of hope, people of courage and tenacity. Who, despite the difficulties, bear encouraging witness for the future."

Jesus was born a migrant. Not only because he came directly from God, our Creator, but because his life was marked by his condition as a stranger: born in a manger surrounded by the warmth of animals, far from his homeland, he fled to Egypt as a political exile, and lived his ministry walking from town to town, often sleeping in the open air of the desert.

He said it himself:

"Foxes have holes and birds of the air have nests, but the Son of Man has nowhere to lay his head."

(Luke 9:58)

It could be interpreted that, although animals have a place to live, He, being the Son of God, has no fixed place to live. Jesus not only understands the pain of the displaced, of the migrant... He also experienced it. He was persecuted by those in power, rejected, condemned for breaking with the established order. His life, in some way, embodies the grief of migration and, at the same time, the greatest act of universal empathy. He became human to walk with us. He died with open arms to save us from sin, embracing all of humanity.

Jesus left behind no riches, no armies, no temples. He left behind a Church that transcended the ages. He left behind a message that broke the internal and external boundaries of our hearts. Among them:

"You shall love the stranger as yourself."

A central transmitter of radical empathy:

"You shall love your neighbor as yourself," even if that other person is of a different culture, a different skin color, a different way of thinking, a different language, a different faith.

This principle remains revolutionary today. Even in countries founded on Christian foundations and with biblical principles such as human respect, migrants are still discriminated against.

Jesus represents the soul's exodus, the departure from comfort to embrace love. The abandonment of ego to walk toward others. The fall into the abyss of society to discover that God dwells there as well.

Jesus is the symbol of the perfect migrant: he carried no baggage, but he brought wisdom. He had no citizenship, but he is the prince of a kingdom not of this world. He owned no property, but he offered eternal inheritances. He didn't speak every language, but his message crossed all tongues. His biography is a map of journeys: from heaven to earth, from Bethlehem to Egypt, from the synagogue to the desert, from the mountain to Golgotha, from death to life.

CHAPTER 13

The new human civilization

In this closing section of this wonderful experience, with which those of us who have experienced migration can surely identify, along with those who haven't, we're going to philosophize a bit. We've already brought the human being through his evolutionary process, also examining our fellow planet members: the non-humans. We could look at a random perspective, a new generation, a new civilization. From that perspective, we'll propose three paths that, as a human race, we could take to reflect and integrate according to our synthesis and way of seeing human existence:

First phase: Return to paradise

Let's reflect a little on the creation of man, what God intended for us—humans and nonhumans alike—when he designed Eden, or Paradise. Paradise is, in a symbolic sense, the sacred origin of the human soul, the place to which we all, even without knowing it, long to return: to return to our paternal home that God made for humanity. Eden was the first territory where man and woman lived without fear, without borders, without pain. It was a perfect and complete place: beauty, food, nature (nonhumans—animals), peace, companionship, purpose.

(Genesis 2:8) "And God planted a garden eastward in Eden, and there he placed the man whom he had formed."

But even in Eden, there was a test of freedom, a charter of values, a covenant, a covenant: not to eat the fruit of the tree of the knowledge of good and evil. It was the only limit God set as a sign of trust. Our parents, Adam and Eve, broke it: they ate the fruit, they ate the apple. They didn't just cross a spiritual line; they crossed the first frontier of the human soul. Pain, frustration, shame, sweat, work, and death were born. And with them, eternal exile:

"You will be a stranger in the land I gave you, and you will earn your living by the sweat of your brow."

Since then, humankind has been a migrant not only geographically but existentially. We search, we wander, we start over. From civilization to civilization: hatred, war, competition, power, envy as a feeling of defeat within the human heart. The first children of our parents, Adam and Eve, were named Cain and Abel. Because of these feelings, which still disrupt our daily lives today, Cain killed his brother Abel, and with him was born God's curse: the first aimless migrant.

Genesis 4:12 "When you till the ground, it will yield no fruit; you will be a fugitive and a vagabond on the earth."

In the societies that followed, God saw that this feeling of evil in man was uncontrollable, he saw that evil on earth was great and that all his thoughts always tended toward evil.

Genesis 6:6, 22 "And God regretted that he had made man, and his heart was troubled. And God said, I will wipe from the face of the earth this humankind that I have created, and also the beasts, the creeping things, and the birds, for I regret that I have made them."

God decided to create the Flood, that is, to send waters over the earth for forty days and forty nights to wipe out every living being under the sky. To cleanse this society and thus give birth to a new, purer one, he then chose Noah, a pure and loyal man, to build the Ark of cypress wood. Noah's Ark would be 150 meters long, 25 meters wide, and 15 meters high, with a total of three floors.

God said to Noah:

"I will make a covenant with you, and you will enter the ark— you and your wife, your sons, and the wives of your three sons with you. You will bring non-humans (animals) into the ark, a pair of every living creature, so that they may survive with you; you will take a male and a female. Of every species of birds, animals, and everything that creeps on the ground, only a pair will enter with you so that they may save their lives. Of clean animals you will take with you seven pairs of each species, each male with its female. Of unclean animals you will take a male with its female."

The good news is that, once the Flood had passed, and everything had returned to the normality that was expected, God said to Noah and his sons:

"I will make a covenant with you and with your descendants after you, and with every living being who is with you."

That is, it also referred to non-humans: domestic animals, birds, and wild beasts; in a word, all the beasts of the earth that have come out of the ark.

Genesis 9:11 "The covenant I make with you is that from now on no living thing will be killed by the waters of a flood, nor will there ever be a flood to destroy the earth."

God places a reminder of that covenant

And he said, "Between you and me, and every living creature that is with you, throughout all generations to come, I set my bow in the clouds as a sign of a covenant with all the earth."

And it's the rainbow of colors we see in the sky. Curiously, we see it so close that when we try to reach it with the intention of touching it, we feel it's far away again; and when we think it's far away, it's close. We estimate that these sensations are homogeneous for both humans and non-humans.

God has been benevolent toward both human and non-human races. We see that He has always protected us, always been there. In this symbiosis between us, we complement each other. We have seen this throughout this study, from different spheres of creation. Our intention is that, through these dialogues—where the primary author is our Creator, God— human society may regain, through reconversion and solidarity, a perspective on where we come from and where we can go. Because God allows human and non-human beings free will, but He also establishes alliances. He is strong and determined: when we fail to fulfill them, we are punished.

We've had many opportunities from Him to confirm this. The question is: are we achieving it? For a good question, a good answer... or the answer is in the question itself: let's reflect.

After the flood, it happens again

Humans, out of control with the construction of the Tower of Babel. At that point in history:

Genesis 11:1-2 "And they all spoke the same language, and they used the same expressions. As people migrated from the east, they found a plain in the region of Shinear, and they settled there."

Humans had a small idea: to build a city with a tower reaching to heaven, with the intention of reaching Him, challenging Him again. Then God said:

Genesis 11:7 "Let us go down and confuse their language there so that they will not understand one another."

What happened next was that different languages were born. That society, seeing that they couldn't understand each other, dispersed across the earth. Each linguistically homogeneous group took their animals—sheep, dogs, and cats—and migrated from that city.

The Bible follows his journey: the call of Abraham, slavery in Egypt, God's liberation of Moses, the Exodus as a manifestation of the first symbol of divine liberation and justice, the forty years of life in the desert, the kings Saul, David, and Solomon. David, as a messianic figure, anticipates the life of Jesus. Solomon builds the temple. Then comes the division of the kingdom and the exile in Babylon. Idolatry, corruption, and decadence emerge. God allows exile as punishment and correction. Hope for the coming of the Messiah is born.

We continue: the major and minor prophets: Isaiah, Jeremiah, Ezekiel, Amos, etc. The return from exile and the rebuilding of the Temple: an attempt at spiritual and moral renewal. But the people continue to fall into legalism. Then comes the domination of foreign empires (Persian, Greek, Roman). Israel falls under the yoke of superpowers. A strong desire for liberation and messianic justice arises. The birth of Jesus and with Him, the Gospels: a new era for humanity.

Connecting the beginning with the end

We want to find in this rationality a point of connection between what God initially intended with the creation of Paradise, Eden, and the biblical message of his final book: the Book of Revelation. We want to connect our original home—Genesis—with the new Jerusalem, which is eternal life.

Thanks to our first parents, Adam and Eve, we earned the worst punishment for disobeying God: death (but not work). Work is a blessing that has made humanity grow.

We can recover the Paradise we lost, that depends on each one of us, to reach the new Jerusalem, heaven itself, a city where there is no crying or pain, where creation is restored and God walks again with his children, as in the original garden:

Revelation 21:1-4 "Then I saw a new heaven and a new earth...and death would be no more, neither mourning nor crying nor pain anymore, for the former things had passed away."

The Bible reveals to us that the deepest migration is not geographical, but spiritual: a return to the lost Paradise, now transformed into a luminous, inclusive, just, and eternal city. Eden was closed by the fiery sword. The New Jerusalem opens its pearly gates to all who believe, hope, and love.

In this migration throughout history, God awaits our cleansing. We are migrants in this life span that each of us occupies on this earth. The migrant's final destiny is to return home, not to the lost garden, but to eternal life, to the rebuilt New Jerusalem, where heaven and earth merge once again and the divine plan is fulfilled: a restored creation, human and nonhuman, reconciled with its Creator.

The ecstasy of migration

It is not an escape, but a collective rebirth. The stranger Jesus is the modern migrant. He is the restored human being. He is the displaced animal. He is the seed that germinates in new soil. We all travel together, one journey, toward a restored civilization, a state where God wants us converted, not by external powers, nor by a spatial conquest, but by an inner and shared transformation.

Second phase: the conquest of Mars

"Let's go to Mars: from the sky everything is more beautiful, let me take you to the stars again, like last night. Let's go to Mars, where no one will come looking for you, neither you nor me. Where everything is quieter and lonelier for the two of us, where there is no one but you and me...
Let's leave the earth full of such shitty people who want to crush us... Let's go on a trip to the stars and to Mars... To forget our piercing problems, let's contemplate the constellations and all our visions... That take away the emptiness we felt on earth... Take my hand and let's leave here... Put on your gray sweater and let's start running away..."

— Song written and performed by Mexican Kevin Kaarl

The conquest of space begins

Perhaps the greatest benefit of the intelligence endowed to humankind... or a new atonement for God, our Creator. It begins a new construction for the conquest of heaven. The baked bricks and asphalt (pitch) used in the construction of the Tower of Babel are once again placed at the door of the furnace. Only we transform them into rockets. The Earth was no longer enough; our gaze was raised to the firmament, thus beginning the most ambitious human migration of the last two centuries: space migration. The conquest of Mars, the red planet.

The species that inhabit the Earth, humans and non-humans, are collapsing it, in general, due to two perspectives:
One, that as a human species, we are contributing to the destruction of the planet—pollution and environmental destruction—and, second, that we are contributing to the destruction of coexistence. It is our great frustrations as human beings that prevent us from living an optimal life.

The idea of moving to another world is to inhabit and create a renewed, clean planet with different minds, where natural resources are not modified, our lives are not augmented, and we live in peace and harmony.

One of the causes of most human death is the food and medicines supplied to us by large laboratories, which don't cure, but rather soothe. Hence, we have diseases that have been unable to progress in their cure. Major research on the subject yields the same results: the way we eat is killing us. What will we eat on Mars? We can work toward that goal, taking care of our health, but that requires a structural change throughout the entire process, throughout the entire value chain, where wealth, distribution channels, and power are reduced.

Ancient humans lived up to 900 years. God established in Genesis 6:3 that humans should not live past the age of 120. We are below average. We are poisoning ourselves with food, plus the frustration of power and war. This is not what our initial conquerors and colonizers of the planet Mars talked about. Their interests are being skewed by other perspectives. But let's focus on that reality, since a fork in the road is beyond our reach.

The space age began in 1957 with Sputnik 1, was humanized in 1961 with Yuri Gagarin, and left its mark on another star in 1969 with Neil Armstrong and Buzz Aldrin.

In the 21st century, Elon Musk is reviving that legacy with a radical vision: to make Mars our second home by 2050, aiming to migrate one million people to this planet. However, this interstellar exodus still faces enormous challenges: Mars's hostile gravity, radiation, and lack of oxygen and food. (Gravity affects our perception of them.)

To address some solutions, the Moon is being looked to as a bridge: a natural platform where humanity can stock up on water, oxygen, and fuel before launching toward the red planet.

The strategy of establishing lunar bases, like the Artemis program and SpaceX's Starship, is not just a logistical one: it's an act of profound migratory continuity. Just as early sailors created coastal colonies to hop from continent to continent, now humans are preparing their bases in space.

Starship, the spacecraft developed by SpaceX, is the most advanced and ambitious space transportation system designed to date, specifically designed for missions to the Moon, Mars, and beyond. It can carry up to 100 people or more than 100 tons of cargo. One Starship can resupply another in orbit to enable longer flights, such as to Mars.

The journey from Earth to the Red Planet can take between six and nine months, depending on the position of Earth and Mars, as they must align every 26 months. The explanation is that Earth and Mars orbit the Sun at different speeds:

- Earth: one orbit every 12 months
- Mars: one orbit every 23 months

So, every 26 months, both planets align so that the distance between them is minimal and the travel path is shortest and most fuel-efficient.
This point is called opposition. During this window, space agencies like NASA and SpaceX can:

- Send ships with lower energy consumption

- Take advantage of the Hohmann transfer trajectory, which is an ellipse that connects both orbits efficiently

If you miss that window, you have to wait another 26 months to try again.

Elon Musk has said that, in the future, hundreds of Starships could depart in organized fleets during the window. Typically, this window could last between 30 and 45 days, depending on:

- the mission
- propulsion technology
- and the exact distance between both planets at that time

Let's navigate through our minds

I invite you to explore our minds, to take a futuristic journey through what it would be like to live on Mars, in a single journey for humans and non-humans. Let's begin:

We believe the first thing we must adapt is our minds. All these feelings we migrants experience, as we've expressed throughout the book, plus the unspoken ones... Everyone knows what they felt when leaving their homeland. Those feelings are indescribable. What goes on inside our souls cannot be described; it is felt within our guts.

Each of us, probably in a different way, experiences our own experiences. There may come a time when our expressions look the same, but they aren't. That's what makes us human.

Some of us have stronger emotional structures, rooted in our being. Others, to a lesser extent. But what is certain is that our essence is formed with a consistency that we often only discover when we face difficult situations. When we demand our entire selves. When we stretch ourselves and expose ourselves to the fullest extent we can give. That submission to risk, which we ultimately resolve, not even we ourselves know the extent of.

In that range, we are similar. It's when we unite, leverage, and merge in the pursuit of what fulfills us, what makes us happy...like empathy, resilience, and compassion, which is a feeling not only of humans but of nonhumans as well.

Coexistence on Mars

Having advanced this consideration, human relationships on Mars could be marked by coexistence in extreme conditions, especially in the early years of colonization. This will have direct effects on tolerance, conflict management, and mental health.

These primary population groups must prepare for isolation, as the risk of tension, confinement, distance from Earth, and group tension increases.

The New Martians

The new Martians must face numerous tests in isolation simulations. They must be trained in stress management, tolerance and frustration, crisis communication skills, resilience, and emotional monitoring routines from Earth. Virtual therapy, artificial intelligence, and augmented reality tools will be used.

The architecture and emotional design of Martian inhabitants will be designed to reduce claustrophobia: artificial lighting that simulates sunlight, spaces for privacy, and environments reminiscent of nature or Earth. Group cohesion will be managed in small, diverse, and cohesive teams, where everyone has a clear purpose. There will be task rotation to avoid monotony, symbolic celebrations, and a shared culture to foster a sense of community.

How will freedom of worship be handled?

Freedom of worship must be a fundamental principle. Religious freedom will be respected. Every person will have the right to practice, express, and live their faith, as long as it does not interfere with the rights of others. Spaces for spiritual and interfaith encounter will be created; instead of separate temples, there will likely initially be multipurpose spaces where different communities can meet, pray, and share rituals.

These centers will promote interfaith dialogue, helping to avoid conflicts and building bridges of understanding. Coexistence in a closed and isolated environment like Mars will require prior and ongoing education in tolerance, diversity, and conflict resolution. Spirituality will be an important tool for psychological well-being, resilience, and connection to the Earth.

What kind of people will initially live on Mars?

What ages and what types of professions?

Initially, individuals will be carefully selected due to the planet's extreme conditions and the technical, psychological, and social challenges. The most likely profiles will include:

- Preferably between 28 and 50 years old, with high physical and psychological performance, and sufficient maturity and professional experience.
- Highly collaborative and emotionally stable people.
- With intensive training in resilience, confinement, multicultural teamwork, and adaptation to hostile environments.

Key professions:

- Aerospace and mechanical engineers: to build and maintain infrastructure and aircraft.
- Planetary scientists, biologists, and geologists: to study the Martian environment and search for life.
- Doctors and psychologists: essential for physical and mental health.
- Agronomists and biologists specializing in biotechnology: to develop crop and food systems.
- Artificial intelligence and robotics technicians: essential in automated environments.
- Energy and sustainability specialists: to ensure the operation of bases powered by solar or nuclear energy.
- Community leaders or human relations experts: for group management and conflict resolution.

As colonization expands, not only scientists and military personnel will be on Mars. Other types of settlers will arrive as well: educators and artists, urban farmers and sustainability technicians, caregivers and nurses...
And what we are in essence: migrants diverse in vocation, ordinary people, seeking second chances in a new world, carrying with us a history and the endless struggle for happiness.

Who travels more, men or women?

NASA and SpaceX promote gender equity in their current programs. For Mars colonization missions, gender balance is sought, as it is crucial for creating sustainable societies. The ratio can approach 50/50.

From a biological and psychological perspective, some research has shown that women tolerate space radiation and prolonged isolation better. In simulations of living together, mixed-gender teams have demonstrated better performance in cooperation and conflict resolution.

How will sex be handled on Mars?

The colonies will establish codes of sexual ethics, as is the case today on space stations. Sex on Mars will not be like it is on Earth. There, human intimacy will have to adapt to a new context of isolation, extreme cooperation, and collective survival.

Sex, as a part of human emotional and biological life, will not disappear, but neither will it be free and uncontrolled. In a closed and isolated environment, sexual relations cannot be experienced as simple encounters without consequences. The emotional impact of each bond will be greater. Therefore, stable relationships based on trust, empathy, and respect will be fostered.

Sexual freedom will be respected in all its diversity: heterosexual, homosexual, monogamous, or consensually open relationships.
But the emphasis will be on emotional maturity. Orientation will not be judged, but rather commitment to group harmony.

Sex in reduced gravity

Sex will be a different experience due to the reduced gravity. Martian gravity is approximately 38% that of Earth. The human body will weigh less, which implies several changes in the way we perceive our bodies and physically interact with others.

Being overweight will no longer be a problem, which can make movements softer or more imprecise if not well controlled. People will likely need to experiment and learn certain sensations, forms of stimulation, and positions, as the body floats, suspended on Mars. That weight we feel when loving, caressing, or simply touching is reduced to a third...and with it, intimacy also changes in rhythm and form.

Omar Albarracín
Which non-humans will accompany us on Mars?

On Mars, it's not just humans who will migrate: the presence of other living beings and non-human life forms will also be key to sustaining the ecosystem and emotional well-being. Let's look at some possibilities:

- Small animals like bees and pollinators: vital to sustaining crops and artificial ecosystems.
- Small fish: for aquaponics, combining plant and fish farming.
- Rodents such as laboratory mice: for medical, genetic and behavioral studies.
- Dogs and cats: possibly at a more advanced stage, very difficult at first; they will serve as emotional companions. It's a great challenge to move them around the space and resources.
- Edible insects: crickets, beetles and worms, for their high protein, low water consumption and ease of reproduction.
- Microorganisms such as bacteria and fungi: to transform waste, purify water, enrich Martian soils, and produce food or medicine.
- Cyanobacteria: help release oxygen and capture CO_2 in closed biohabitats.
- Essential plants: fast-growing vegetables such as lettuce, potatoes, spinach, tomatoes, basil, wheat, and rice.

Artificial intelligences and robots will be the first non-humans to arrive and work on Mars: for habitat construction, health monitoring, general maintenance, and human companionship. Some humanoids will have social duties: escorting, conversing, monitoring, or facilitating household chores. These non-humans will be an integral part of an interplanetary symbiosis, serving as a fulcrum for the human Martian community.

Third phase: The society of the future

The best society of the future, to which we must all migrate, is the one that is born within each of us, the one we radiate to others. It is born from our very being, contributing to building a more conscious society, better human beings, more empathetic, one that understands that this transformation begins from within. Let us understand how symbiosis works among us humans in our own daily relationships, and let us also be inclusive of non-humans, who are part of us.

When we anchor these behaviors in each of us and share them as a norm of life, they immediately become collective. To that extent, it's easier to make the necessary changes to our deepest frustrations; therefore, they may be easier to transform. We don't need to flee to survive, no matter what the circumstances. Perhaps that's not the only option; perhaps it's worth trying, trying again, in our own spaces where we can move freely to share, contribute, learn, and grow.

From another perspective, changes must be made to the structures that control societies and that were created for our own protection:

- Politics must cease to be the domain of a few and their personal interests and become what it truly represents: a discipline that seeks to unravel and understand people's ideas, institutions, and the behavior of social groups. It must become a true tool for participation and equity.
- The economy must put human beings and nature above capital, recognizing that work has dignity and that no one should live in hunger or fear.
- The society of the future must understand that nonhumans are not resources, but partners in this shared existence, where we learn from them cooperation, empathy, compassion, and their way of living in harmony.
- The spirituality and purpose of each of us must grow, because spirituality does not divide, but unites. Respect for others becomes part of the social fabric, as do love, solidarity, gratitude, and compassion.
- Promote education to continue growing as a society. Education is the essential pillar of human growth in the future, not only to transmit knowledge, but to transform consciences, awaken empathy, and build critical, free, and committed citizens. Education reconnects us with human beings and nonhumans, makes us more sensitive, restores our essence, and teaches us to coexist, not to dominate. It becomes the most powerful tool for creating a better future.

- Social justice and equity: We clearly see what is currently happening with migration, how we are often treated as criminals without being criminals, without due process, without the right to defend ourselves. We cannot be marginalized in any social setting as human beings. We have the right to live freely, to have our rights respected, and to be free from violence, exploitation, and exclusion.

Throughout history, society has created its own filters: the primitive system, ancient society, feudalism... all the way to the capitalist system. Other political systems, such as communism or socialism, are unproven social theories. It's not worth focusing on them even a little.

An ideal capitalist system, for a balanced society, is one that maintains innovation, wealth equity, and economic freedom, ensuring its excesses are corrected, protecting the most vulnerable, and ensuring the sustainability of the planet. These well-conditioned variables mean that the need for human migration, and indeed, non-human migration, is less likely to be encouraged.

Symbiosis occurs in both positive and negative ways. One is relevant to the other. The true essence of the metaphor "Immigrants don't eat dogs or cats" is that humans and non-humans coexist with mutual respect and care, where they are not allowed to be negatively violated.

We don't need another planet. We need another humanity. A humanity that each of us builds, from within ourselves. It's building the lost paradise.

Scan the following QR code by Bayron Omar Albarracín Monsalve:

Conclusion

A migrant truth that challenges history

This book isn't born from the comfort of a classroom or from the distance of an academic life. It's born from the depths of my soul. From the ground I walk on when I travel without papers. From the heart that breaks when I leave a country and is slowly rebuilt with the faith of someone who knows they're alive for something greater.

Here you won't find cold theories or soulless numbers. Here you will find humanity. Words with scars. Questions that still bleed. And also answers woven with dignity. Because talking about migration isn't just talking about politics or economics: it's talking about the human soul and its infinite capacity to endure, to transform, to be reborn.

Migration, we have discovered together, is not a crisis: it is an expression of courage. It is not a threat: it is an opportunity for collective evolution. It is the silent cry of millions who cross deserts, seas, cities, and offices, not out of choice, but out of necessity. And yet, they do so with their heads held high, their hearts full of stories, and their souls stretched out in service to a new land.

This book also aims to open the door to a forgotten concept: symbiosis. That natural relationship between different beings that, rather than destroying each other, complement each other. Humans and nonhumans. Migrants and locals. Science and spirituality. Because only through this deep connection can we build a more just and conscious civilization.

"Immigrants don't eat dogs or cats" isn't a defensive phrase; it's a mirror. A reflection of the absurdity of prejudice and the power of redefinition. It's a way of saying: look at me carefully, because I'm not what you fear. I'm what you need to remember. I am humanity in motion. I am the memory of struggle. I am the possibility of a new world.

Today, more than ever, the entire planet is in motion. Borders become walls or bridges. The decisions of a few affect millions. That's why this book is also a call. To governments. To citizens. To migrants. To the animals who walk beside us. To the consciences that no longer want to sleep. To all those who know that another way of living—and migrating—is possible.

Because migration doesn't stop. But it can be transformed. It can stop hurting so much. It can become a ritual of rebirth. A dance of cultures. A meaningful journey.

This book ends. But the journey is just beginning. Always by the hand of GOD.

Epilogue

Immigrants don't eat dogs or cats.
An open letter to humanity.

This book is neither an autobiography nor a doctoral thesis. It was not written in the comfort of a library or from the distance of a cold observer. It was born with hands full of dirt, with feet tired from walking, with a soul torn and rebuilt a thousand times over. It was written from the depths of experience, where words are no longer theory, but living flesh.

I'm not a professional writer. I'm something more dangerous, freer, more real: I'm a lucid witness to migration as a wound and a blessing. I'm one of the millions of bodies that have crossed borders with more dreams than papers. I'm one of those who don't fit into political speeches or news headlines. I'm one of those who never give up.

This book is an act of resistance and tenderness.
It's a cry, but it's also a caress.
It's a trench, but it's also an altar.

This book addresses not only the human exodus, but also the non-human one. Because if there's one thing we've lacked as a civilization, it's recognizing that we don't migrate alone: animals, ecosystems, trees, and oceans have also been displaced. This book is an act of poetic justice for all of them.

We've been called illegals, invaders, strangers, dangerous. But we know the truth: we are brave, we are sowers of hope.

Migrating isn't fleeing.
Migrating is reinventing yourself. It's facing death and continuing onward. It's leaving behind a land that denied us bread and embracing a heaven we haven't yet seen.

It's loving life so deeply that we're willing to start over, without guarantees, without certainties, only with faith.

This book doesn't offer easy answers. It offers urgent questions:
What kind of world are we building? Why have we confused security with rejection? When will we understand that no one leaves home unless it's out of necessity? What would a world look like where migration isn't synonymous with pain, but with encounter?

I didn't write this to impress. I wrote it to awaken.
So that we can look into each other's eyes. So that we can remember what's essential. That we are one. That we are many. That we are the same species, even if we speak different languages or have different skin colors. And that nonhumans aren't here to serve us, but to share life with us.

"Immigrants Don't Eat Dogs or Cats" is more than a provocative title. It's a metaphor.
It's a response to ignorance, prejudice, and racism disguised as humor. It's a vibrant defense of the right to exist, to search, to begin again without being humiliated. It's a prayer for all those who have died crossing rivers, deserts, jungles, and seas. It's a tribute to those who still wait. And it's a declaration of love for those who no longer have the strength to speak.

And if I hope this book has planted anything in you, it's awareness.
Not pity. Not guilt.
Awareness.
That flame that transforms your gaze, that humanizes your judgment, that compels you to act.

Thank you for joining me on this journey.
Thank you for reading with your heart.
Thank you for understanding that migration isn't just a physical experience: it's spiritual, emotional, symbolic, interplanetary, and evolutionary.

Because we all migrate, even without moving. We migrate every time we leave behind an old version of ourselves.
We migrate every time we decide to grow.
We migrate when we choose love over fear.

And when all this is over—when the dust of wars and exiles settles—
something stronger than hatred, power, and unjust laws will remain:
the truth of who we were, and what we chose to be.

Because in the end, we didn't come to conquer territories, but to expand our humanity.
And we will.
With a suitcase full of dreams. With a willing heart. And with the absolute certainty that God walks beside us.

And then you'll understand:
We don't eat dogs.
We don't eat cats.
We feed on hope. And we sow dignity where others sow fear.

Thank you for walking with me.
This journey is just beginning.

— *Migrant author, human, unrepeatable, always by the hand of God*

Omar Albarracín

Glossary

Emotional isolation:
A state of emotional disconnection experienced by an immigrant when deprived of their ties, language, and culture in a new territory.

Non-human animal:
A term that recognizes the sensitivity, intelligence, and emotions of animals, differentiating them from humans without stripping them of their value. In this book, they are traveling companions and a mirror of the migratory experience.

The Arc of the Covenant (Rainbow):
A spiritual symbol of hope, inclusion, and a pact between the Creator and all living species, human and nonhuman. It represents the promise of a new beginning after exile or chaos.

Biohabitat:
A living space designed to sustain life in extreme locations (such as Mars) where humans, plants, microorganisms, and technologies coexist symbiotically.

Culture of origin:
System of beliefs, values, customs, symbols, language, and ties that define the collective soul of a community before the migration process.

Migratory grief:
The profound emotional process experienced by a person upon leaving their country, their land, their language, their loved ones, and their social status. In Joseba Achotegui's model, it is identified in seven simultaneous grief processes.

Migratory ecstasy:
A heightened phase of spiritual, emotional, and social transformation

that can arise after the suffering of migration. It is the blossoming of the soul after the darkness of exile.

Migrant identity:
The fusion of what we were with what we are becoming in the host country. An identity in transit, reconstructed with scars and resilience.

Learned helplessness:
A psychological state in which migrants feel that no matter what they do, nothing will change. It arises from repeated failure in the face of a system that doesn't welcome or listen to them.

Interculturality:
A respectful, dynamic, and transformative encounter between different cultures, which does not seek to homogenize, but rather to enrich coexistence through mutual recognition.

Jesus the Stranger:
Symbol of the sacred migrant who embodies in his life the experience of exile, rejection, and rebirth. In this book, Jesus is presented as the traveling companion of every landless traveler.

Migrant neurodiversity:
Recognition that each person processes their migration experience uniquely, according to their emotional makeup, their biography, and their connections to nonhumans.

Non-human migrants:
Animals, microorganisms, plants, and technologies that accompany the human exodus. They are part of the evolutionary symbiosis and the new civilization.

Lost Paradise:
Symbol of the sacred and harmonious origin that was shattered by disobedience or separation. In the migrant context, it represents what we leave behind and what we unconsciously wish to rebuild.

Universal neighbor:
A spiritual concept that defines the other as an extension of oneself,

regardless of nationality, race, language, or creed. Migrating with love is recognizing the divinity of others.

Migrant resilience:

The extraordinary capacity to adapt, rebuild, and flourish in adverse contexts. It's not just about surviving; it's about being reborn with dignity and purpose.

Symbiosis:

A relationship of interdependence and mutual benefit between living beings. This book advocates an emotional and spiritual symbiosis between humans and nonhumans on the migratory journey.

Ulysses Syndrome:

An extreme stress disorder that affects many vulnerable immigrants. Named after the Greek hero Ulysses, who endured numerous trials to return home.

Emotional territory:

A symbolic space inhabited by memories, smells, tastes, words, and emotions. It doesn't always have a physical geography. Migrating also means losing and rebuilding that territory.

Ulysses (archetype):

A mythical figure of the migrant who, after many trials, returns transformed. In this book, Ulysses is a symbol of the soul that never gives up in its search for an inner home.

Bibliography

Achotegui, J. (2005). *Immigrant depression: Ulysses syndrome.* University of Barcelona.

Achotegui, J. (2010). *Migratory Intelligence* . Atenea Foundation.

Achotegui, J. (2010, October 30 - November 1). *World Congress of Transcultural Psychiatry: Migration and Mental Health in the 21st Century.* World Psychiatric Association.

American Immigration Council. (2024). *Immigrant entrepreneurs: Creating jobs and strengthening the economy.* https://www.americanimmigrationcouncil.org/

Jerusalem Bible. (Latest ed.). Bible Society.

Frankl, V.E. (1946). *Man's Search for Meaning.* Herder Editorial.

Hernández, L. (2017). *The Illusion of the American Dream.* Self-published.

Jaramillo, C. (2020). *The Metabolic Miracle.* Editorial Planeta.

Jaramillo, C. (2022). *Anti-stress: The art of eating well to feel good.* Grijalbo.

Karen, J. (n.d.). *Racism in the Common Sense.* [Excerpt quoted by Achotegui].

POT. (2024). *Artemis program documentation.* National Aeronautics and Space Administration. https://www.nasa.gov/

SpaceX. (2024). *Starship architecture and Mars colonization white papers.* https://www.spacex.com/

Selye, H. (1956). *The stress of life.* McGraw-Hill.

UNESCO. (2023). *Interculturality, migration and education.* United Nations Educational, Scientific and Cultural Organization. https://unesdoc.unesco.org/

UNESCO. (2019). *The Value of Cultural Diversity.* https://unesdoc.unesco.org/

Vatican. (2013–2024). *Messages of Pope Francis on Migration.* Pontifical Commission for Migrants and Refugees. https://migrants-refugees.va/

About the author

Omar Octavio Albarracín Prieto, 55, Colombian, is a passionate researcher of human behavior with a solid track record in the business world. Married and a father of three, he has dedicated his life to his family, professional development, and the exploration of human potential.

A graduate in Business Administration from Francisco de Paula Santander University—one of the top ten academic institutions in Colombia—Omar has specialized in management indicators and internal control, standing out for his strategic, analytical, and human approach in each of his roles.

With over 34 years of experience in the commercial sector, his career includes milestones such as:

- Sales consultant for 7 years in the area of delivery sales of household goods.
- Corporate sales advisor at Celumóvil SA, a pioneering mobile phone company in Colombia, where he also served as a regional delegate to the national board of his workers' cooperative.

- Sub-distributor for Colombia for 7 years for Bellsouth, one of the most influential American telecommunications companies.
- Exclusive national distributor for 11 years of Movistar Colombia, part of Telefónica Móviles of Spain.

In recent years, it has expanded its global reach as an importer of Colombian handicrafts and clothing to the United States, managing wholesale and retail sales through 2023.

Since then, he has redirected his vocation toward the study of human behavior, writing, and the development of social, cultural, and migration awareness. In April 2024, he published his first book, "The Lion King in Business – Teamwork," a powerful analogy between business leadership and the wisdom of nature.

He is currently pursuing a master's degree in Human Resources at the University of Florida (UTH) and has completed her second book: **"Immigrants Don't Eat Dogs or Cats – Symbiosis of Migration: Humans and Non-Humans, One Journey**," a provocative and transformative work that seeks to build bridges of empathy between species, cultures, and realities.

His greatest desire as a human being is to continue learning to transmit knowledge, raise awareness, and contribute to the evolution of collective thought.

Author Contact

Omar Octavio Albarracín Prieto
♟ Colombian resident in the U.S.
📚 Author of *"The Lion King in Business – Teamwork"* and *"Immigrants Don't Eat Dogs or Cats"*

📩 Direct contact

✉ **Email** : indígena.store.colombia@gmail.com

🔗 Social networks

🖼 **Facebook** : trainer omar albarracin
📷 **Instagram** : @traineromaralbarracin
🦉 **Twitter/X** : @OmarAlbarracin_
💼 **LinkedIn** : linkedin.com/in/omaralbarracin
🎥 **YouTube (author's channel)** : trainer Omar Albarracin

For interviews, conferences, workshops, or collaborations , you can write directly to their email or send a private message on their official social media channels.

www.ingramcontent.com/pod-product-compliance
Lightning Source LLC
Chambersburg PA
CBHW051732020426

42333CB00014B/1279